FACILITIES MANAGEMENT

THE CHANDOS SERIES ON CONSTRUCTION & FACILITIES

FACILITIES MANAGEMENT

A Strategy For Success

Trevor Payne

Chandos Publishing (Oxford) Limited

ISBN 1 902375 35 1

Chandos Publishing (Oxford) Limited
Chandos House
5 & 6 Steadys Lane
Stanton Harcourt
Oxford OX8 1RL
England

Tel: 01865 882727 Fax: 01865 884448
Email: sales@chandospublishing.com
www.chandospublishing.com

Printed in England

Contents

Foreword

Professions and new business approaches have much in common with species in an ecosystem. They occupy distinct niches. In the UK surveyors, in one variant or another, have captured the niche for a variety of transfers involving an item of value, from land to fine art. Across the Channel Europeans have no translation for the word 'surveyor'. Other professions occupy the equivalent economic niches.

FM as a profession, an area of management practice and an area of business practice is still in the throes of carving – and defining – its own niche, one which draws from pure organisational management and the skills of different 'property', 'engineering' and service professions. Meanwhile it is developing as an area of management practice and is gaining, slowly, a place at the top table of organisations in different sectors.

Among the sectors where the achievement and demonstration of that strategic contribution is well advanced is the UK's National Health Service, where over the last six years I have had the pleasure of seeing the ideas of this book take shape. FM, at this level, is not another word for office design, or planned maintenance, or building support systems, or cleaning contracts, or . . ., although the Facilities Director must ensure that his or her organisation receives those services and more, in ways that enhance their delivery of either shareholder or – as in the NHS – taxpayer value. It means he or she thinking, not in terms of the patterns developed during early professional training and practice, but in terms of ensuring 'customers' who are part of the service experience receive what they need – and what they need may not be what they want, or recognise they need.

Trevor Payne is one of that new breed, developing the new FM role, not perhaps by grand prior design but because it works and delivers better value in practice. He is not the only FD, in or beyond the NHS, who is doing these things. He is the first to also seek to encapsulate what he does. Others, including his peers or his readers, might put those challenges differently or put an altered emphasis on solutions, but that is as it should be for there is no one best answer in FM, only a better way of thinking about it. Strategies actually followed in organisations emerge, to paraphrase Henry Mintzberg, as a *pattern in a stream of decisions*. Success derives from appreciating, and where necessary shifting, those patterns.

Facilities Management – A Strategy for Success should appeal both to the author's peers, those involved in crafting new strategic patterns in FM, and to the next generation, those preparing themselves for their own place in the strategic limelight.

Professor If Price

Co-Director, Facilities Management Graduate Centre

Sheffield Hallam University

Preface

The vast majority of today's facilities managers and practising FM professionals that are currently in post or working in the industry all over the world did not originally set out from school, college or university with their life's ambition focused on becoming a facilities manager. FM training, professional development and career paths are relatively new to the profession – so why so many facilities managers and why now? The provision of facilities (hotel/support services) have by and large always been delivered within most organisations – possibly provided by a number of departments, controlled by a number of different managers, often with services being provided within rigid demarcation boundaries, which locked in inefficiency and stifled service innovation. Services were delivered in a fragmented, often inconsistent manner, historically operating in the reactive rather than proactive mode. Clearly this situation had to change.

So what makes a facilities manager? Successful facilities service delivery demands a range of core management competencies – many of which are learned on the job and gained from experience.

There is no mould, preferred blueprint or production line designed to produce or train a facilities manager. Each manager will arrive in post with a portfolio of experience and training – only some of which will be relevant to the tasks placed before them. Essentially facilities managers are co-ordinators – people who can get the job done – translating the big picture painted by the organisation's strategy into sharp-end service delivery/support mechanisms that are designed to underpin the work processes of the organisation. Often facilities managers are steering the ship with one eye on the shifting horizon and the other eye looking over their shoulder, dealing with the here and now and the 'what may become'. An extensive management toolkit is required to service the task.

This book will outline the key pointers for developing the FM service. A unique set of skills are required to manage facilities and this book will highlight and reinforce the need for facilities managers to develop an FM strategy designed to guide the facilities service provision in the most appropriate manner, to fully complement organisational strategy, whilst at the same time ensuring that performance monitoring systems and communication channels are developed and operated to check that service provision is delivered as specified and agreed.

AIMS OF THE PUBLICATION

The aim of this book is to serve as a useful and useable reference document for facilities professionals which should become well thumbed and ultimately be more at home on the office desk than sat collecting dust on the office shelf. The intention is that this book should be regarded as a useful, digestible reference text for a range of facilities practitioners covering a variety of professional backgrounds. The chapters and sections have been developed to highlight important topic areas, while relevant details are summarised into useful bullet point lists of key pointers drawn from the text for quick reference. This book is aimed at giving guidance on pertinent FM issues, presented in a format that is not aimed at any particular professional discipline or method of service delivery. The topics that are to be discussed will be of equal relevance and importance to facilities managers who have perhaps originally been trained in professions such as Quantity Surveying, Architecture or Engineering who have taken on a wider and broader remit for a range of operational facilities issues, as well as office managers or Human Resource managers who may also find themselves with the responsibility for managing a facilities portfolio (perhaps in a smaller organisation or organisations that recognise that management of change and associated personnel skills drive their organisation's agendas). Each chapter will outline key FM topics that will support the generalist approach to facilities management. Therefore this publication will attempt to pitch the level of guidance to be relevant to both the technical/professional manager and to the traditional or general manager/administrator in order to support:

- managers new to FM (who are aware of the concept and potential benefits of FM) but feel exposed as aspects of their new remit seem alien to them and remote from their skill base;

- practising FM professionals with specialist background in a particular area – wishing to expand their knowledge across the broad FM remit;

- FM students completing postgraduate training or modular training in areas of FM professional competence.

This book will serve to identify the main issues that may face a facilities manager who is new in post, is new to the organisation or is relatively new to certain aspects of facilities management. This book will:

- outline how to develop a strategy to take the service forward;

- stress the importance of customer focus;

- focus on key areas of service delivery;

- look at the important aspects of facilities performance and monitoring.

The final chapter outlines the possible challenges and future directions for the facilities profession – which effectively may take managers outside of their comfort zones or current knowledge base. The basket of FM services is constantly expanding (it is not unusual for services to be 'tagged' onto the facilities provision because they do not neatly fit elsewhere within the make up of the organisation). This approach to the growth of the FM service portfolio (which could be likened to placing a sponge beneath a dripping tap) can bring benefits, but all too often the service portfolio or basket of services grows without the facilities manager having a full and sufficient working knowledge or operational grasp of the total range of services that they are responsible for – and with little or no time to obtain the required knowledge in detail.

The following chapters outline and detail what are considered to be essential areas for developing and taking forward the facilities management service provision. A framework of key pointers will be developed – which will be relevant to both public and private service providers and which is of equal relevance to both in-house teams and contract service providers. A considerable amount of useful and very relevant research exists and is available within the public domain as well as reference material. Both research and reference data will be referred to in each chapter where appropriate in order to support points raised.

This book will help to provide answers to questions such as:

- 'Who are the true customers of facilities services?'

- 'How does the newly appointed facilities manager go about the task of developing the facilities management service?'

- 'Input or output service specification?'

- 'What and how should services be monitored' – who should do it?

The practice of facilities management has been adopted within and implemented across a wide range of organisations, covering a broad spectrum of both public and private sector companies varying in both size and complexity, with many permutations of service delivery and scope of services which may also represent a mixture of in-house and contract service providers delivering services under the facilities banner.

Yet suprisingly, many managers and organisations do not understand fully the concept or the benefits associated with the facilities management approach.

The Author

Trevor Payne is the Head of Facilities at one of the largest acute teaching hospitals in the UK which has an international reputation as a centre of excellence.

He has a professional engineering background having trained in both Electrical and Plant Engineering, and subsequently took an MSc in Facilities Management at CFM, Strathclyde Graduate Business School, graduating in 1998.

He is a member of the BIFM and a number of national learning sets and benchmarking clubs. Trevor is also an active member of HEFMA (Healthcare Estates & Facilities Management Association) and is a member of the national training and development sub-group; he has also submitted papers for their yearbook.

Trevor is responsible for a wide range of facilities services covering four diverse hospital sites within a mixed economy of in-house and outsourced providers. He has particular interest in performance monitoring, benchmarking and facilities strategy and is currently working on best value and a healthcare PFI project.

He regularly presents papers at seminars and conferences on matters relating to Facilities Management and is a member of the editorial board of the journal *Facilities Management*.

Trevor has just finished working on an international healthcare project that took him to Morocco and Bulgaria and has been invited to present a paper in Sydney Australia in the autumn of 2000.

Introduction

The growth of facilities management in the United Kingdom over the past decade has been rapid and its effects have been far-reaching. The facilities profession has developed from an early formative stage in the late eighties, through to a rapid growth phase which took place during the mid-nineties. Currently facilities management is reaching a level of maturity that is poised to take it forward and guide it through the first years of the new millennium. The contract facilities service providers have gone through a metamorphic change – many facilities companies have been acquired and merged with large construction firms in an attempt to 'buy in' the facilities operating expertise. Traditional cleaning contractors have acquired catering contract companies and car parking and security service providers have acquired cleaning companies and so on. The overall result has been the emergence of a 'super league' of facilities providers who are able to cover the broad remit of facilities management in a comprehensive 'cradle to grave' approach. FM providers and consortium companies now have the ability to design, build, finance and operate buildings (DBFO) over their planned life cycle (a truly strategic step enabling DBFO consortia to influence and 'design out' maintenance and cleaning or logistical operational problems). These super league teams are also positioning themselves as consortium partners for Private Finance Initiative (PFI) deals which look set to secure FM operating contracts for periods of 25–40 years (a number of FM companies already have some limited equity tied up in PFI deals). Some of these providers are now poised to take on global FM (a number of forward-thinking service providers are already working across global time zones and continents).

Facilities management has come a long way in a relatively short period of time but there is still destined to be more change, particularly if facilities are to fully support the anticipated radical changes in the property and construction industries that have been predicted. The manner in which facilities management has evolved and developed has by necessity involved and incorporated professionals attracted from a wide catchment of professional disciplines and backgrounds – all of whom are key to the management of facilities services:

- property and the built environment play a key role and this has required the professional skills of architects, legal services, space planners and quantity surveyors;

- the way that people interact with the built environment has required the input of human resources professionals, building services and environmental engineers;

13

- the technical expertise of technical and maintenance staff;

- the processes that take place within buildings such as catering, cleaning, security, mail room, reprographics (soft FM etc.) has required input and practical operational management from a range of specialist professional backgrounds – the list goes on and on.

And we must not forget the overriding management of risk across all these disciplines. This varied assortment of professional and management skills coupled with the merging or blurring of traditional professional boundaries and the pressure to downsize the organisation (to flatten management hierarchy) has spawned a new breed – 'the facilities manager'.

The BIFM (British Institute of Facilities Management) survey of facilities managers' responsibilities (September 1999) outlined some interesting data with respect to membership profile, job profile, qualifications, reporting lines, etc. Literal interpretation of the survey data identified the nature of 'FM man' as

> a 45-year-old man, directly employed by the facility user. He reports to a director or senior manager yet earns a relatively low £30K per year considering the fact that he holds such a responsible position. He does, however, enjoy a good benefits package including a company car. He doesn't hold a relevant professional qualification, nor is he a graduate. Most of his training has involved short courses and on-the-job training, yet he is responsible for a wide range of tasks from building maintenance to space planning and health & safety. (Eltringham, 1999)

The survey data and responses (90% male) do not reflect the current state of the market, which boasts many more female facilities managers, it also does not represent the make up and market trends of FM outside of the BIFM membership. The above vision of the facilities manager does, however, highlight a number of key points relevant to the general FM spectrum:

- employment trends – in-house or outsourced;

- reporting line to the board – facilities strategy;

- status of FM within the organisation;

- professional background/training;

- wide range of management tasks (basket of services).

The new breed of facilities manager will in all probability be responsible for a broad range of services most of which will sit outside of their original professional discipline or the area of expertise that they trained in. It is now commonplace for quantity surveyors, architects, maintenance engineers, office managers, catering managers and human resource managers to be responsible for the delivery of the full range of facilities services in their particular organisation. The BIFM survey indicates that over 60% of the respondents are managing facilities in corporate office locations or multi-site office space. Therefore building services knowledge or a catering background may not be at the top of the list when selecting a facilities manager to co-ordinate facilities functions within the office environment. Management of people, management of change and management of space may well rank higher in terms of priority with the view that specific expertise can be bought in on contract to fulfil specific requirements or to complete a particular project.

This market development widens the entry level to FM with respect to professional background. FM is all about management and co-ordination and as the market and the profession develops further there will be a move towards recognised management skills and FM qualifications, underpinned by the attainment of knowledge in core competencies in order to develop a recognised toolbox of professional FM skills. Undoubtedly this will lead to facilities managers often learning in post and continuing their professional development to support the wide range of services they may find themselves managing. Due to this basket of services responsibility, facilities managers will find themselves adapting to the role of a generalist rather than a specialist, often knowing a little about a lot of service specialities – but with expert knowledge of only a few. In order to address this potential knowledge gap this publication is intended to draw together knowledge on key areas of facilities management. It will not go back over old ground by mapping the roots of FM development, nor will it dwell on the first principles of the facilities approach, but it will focus on key factors that are essential to take the FM provision forward in a successful manner – highlighting some of the core competencies that are eluded to above.

Current trends and innovations that are destined to enhance the way that facilities are managed will be highlighted and discussed. Because facilities management covers such a broad remit this publication cannot go into great depth on each of the key pointers outlined later in the text – each area really warrants its own dedicated volume. Further reading and linked research will be outlined along with Internet sites/contacts which support in detail the issues being outlined. It is designed to highlight the major building blocks upon which a robust facilities service can be constructed. Due to the range and complexity of FM services this book will not focus on the operational detail of service provision for discrete specialities such as catering, cleaning and security, though a basic overview of maintenance planning will be outlined in Chapter 5. Specialist knowledge or support for these areas will need to be obtained in greater depth by the facilities manager but this book will develop an overarching framework that will support the provision of a range of such services in a cohesive manner.

Many definitions of facilities management exist but they are all basically variations on a theme. For the purpose clarification, the following definition of FM will be used and expanded upon in this publication:

> *The practise of co-ordinating the physical workplace with the people and work of an organisation; [it] integrates the principles of business administration, architecture, and the behavioural and engineering science.* (NHS Estates, 1996:3)

This publication will not redefine the concept of facilities management, but it will attempt to explore the key role that facilities management plays within the organisation and will summarise the necessary steps required to make facilities management a success.

CHAPTER 1

Facilities Strategy

CORE *v* NON-CORE ACTIVITY

The traditional view of facilities management (FM) has been that of a non-core or pure support function which is often seen to be at arm's length to the main thrust or activities of the organisation. Certainly in the early days of FM much emphasis was placed upon facilities taking control of and managing all of the non-critical or non-core functions – which would then enable the organisation to focus on the main business agenda and the core issues that it might be facing. Clearly there are benefits relating to cost, staffing and management overheads associated with combining the management of support functions under one facilities umbrella. Additional benefit is achieved by breaking down traditional demarcation boundaries and combining service functions in an innovative manner – cutting out duplication and wasteful practice. Increasingly organisations are now beginning to realise the true potential of FM services and recognise that they are more than just pure support functions that are limited to operational service delivery. The evolving nature of FM and the maturity of its approach – which is grounded in the experience of a buoyant and growing profession, has begun to ensure that a strategic FM dimension is now a requirement for all successful and forward-thinking organisations. This has largely been driven by the realisation of the cost of FM services and the potential impact to the bottom line. The effective communication of the benefits that a facilities strategy can bring can only serve to move facilities and its profile up to another level within the organisation. For facilities to develop a truly comprehensive and successful strategy the facilities manager must develop an appreciation of the core activities of the host organisation so that facilities are able to influence directly and indirectly the organisational strategy (this strategic dimension is discussed in further detail later in this chapter). This suggests that facilities need to develop shared values and synergy in order to align themselves with the host organisation – in order, that is, to be considered a truly proactive management function.

If the operational function of most organisations were to be analysed and the elements of its processes and sub-processes described and portrayed as a supply chain which mapped all of the functions (from input to output) of the organisation's activities, then a number of the key links in the chain described would be provided and managed by the facilities function. In its best operational mode facilities management could be described as the 'glue' that holds the organisation together and enables it to produce its product in a seamless manner. The range, nature and complexity of the support that facilities offers to the organisation touches and impacts upon all levels (from the top to the bottom) of the organisational hierarchy and the services could equally be regarded as vital enabling functions – in some instances the FM provision could be viewed as 'more core' rather than non-core. In most forward looking organisations there is an appreciation at a senior management level of the contribution that a well managed and effective FM service provision can provide, ensuring that a 100% focus is placed on the support of business activities of the organisation. This will be explored in more detail later in this chapter which focuses in on the development of a facilities strategy.

SERVICE DELIVERY

There are no 'off the peg' solutions to the provision of facilities management. The portfolio of services and the range of options relating to the various combinations of service delivery have sparked discussion and debate over the merits of certain modes of service delivery such as:

- in-house provision (all services provided by directly employed staff) *v* contract service provision (outsourcing – contractors providing services previously provided by in-house teams);

- single service/single source contracts (single/separate contracts for each service – with the overall portfolio managed by the facilities manager or managing agent/consultant) *v* multi-service contract clusters (contracts merged, i.e. portering and housekeeping, or car parking and security managed by the facilities manager or managing agent/consultant);

- total facilities management contract (TFM) – one contractor manages and controls the entire facilities portfolio including all subcontractor service providers.

The final decision regarding which approach to take will ultimately depend on a range of circumstances pertaining to the organisation that exist at the time of setting up the facilities portfolio – each organisation or each site will have its own unique requirement – one size does not fit all.

'Outsourced', in-sourced', 'downsized', 'delayered' or 'right-sized' – the late eighties and early nineties have been the era of the changing organisation where 'out' is in, organisational hierarchy and management structures are flat and the customer is king. The traditional models of the 'organisation' as it previously existed have been reshaped – its hierarchy and structure have been pulled apart, reconfigured and reassembled thus ensuring each component part is necessary and required and adds value to the delivered product. There has been a steady move away from the traditional methods of service delivery which in the past served to protect and support the practice of operating within controlled trade demarcation boundaries. These boundaries or service interface points between trade groups, staff groups and contractors are steadily being eroded as service providers strive for the 'seamless' approach to service delivery in which service provision bridges the gaps between trade groups that previously existed – and to a large extent remained unquestioned and unchallenged. It is in this remodelling that one of the key benefits of the facilities approach lays. Stripping out the inflexible barriers of demarcation can allow true innovation to be developed with respect to how services can be provided, and with this approach inefficiency can be eliminated. Individuals can have more rewarding and more satisfying jobs that provide interest, flexibility and a degree of staff empowerment. True success in this approach rests relies upon clarity, training, flexibility and commitment with respect to the definition of boundaries of individual roles. This chapter will outline the need to develop an effective facilities strategy which maps the planned development of the facilities service provision in a controlled and logical manner. The concept of facilities management as an organisational change driver will be discussed – reflecting on the current climate of churn within organisations and the need to co-ordinate activity so that focus on the core elements of the business can be maintained to ensure that best value is achieved. This chapter will focus on 're-engineering the organisation', and consider the benefits that can be gained from taking a step back and looking in on the organisation and the way that it operates. Linked with this is the requirement to develop a facilities strategy that is designed to fit in with the organisational aims of the host company. Guidance on the strategic viewpoint of contracting and outsourcing will be outlined. The advantages and disadvantages of the various options with regard to packaging service elements (contract bundling) with respect to single service suppliers or total FM contract options will be explored. Current thinking on effective contract duration will also be detailed.

The need to develop organisational synergy between the FM function and the organisation that it services will be discussed – this will include the identification and development of shared values and goals to ensure that the support network is operating in parallel with the direction of the host company.

DEVELOPING AN FM STRATEGY

As facilities management has evolved and developed within organisations there has been a steady realisation of the benefits (tangible and intangible) that can be obtained from effective management of FM services. If facilities managers and facilities professionals are to be truly regarded as 'players' within the organisation then it is essential for the facilities manager to develop a facilities strategy which should map over a stated period of time how the FM services will be reviewed, re-engineered or moulded to best support the needs of the host organisation. The strategy should ideally consist of three strategic elements that build upon the current level of provision (the strategic start point) and should map short-, medium- and long-term goals and targets and give direction for facilities over the stated period. If the strategy is to be of any real value then it must reflect the aims and ambitions of the organisation that is designed to support. The facilities strategy must clearly complement the overriding business strategy of the host organisation and this can only happen if the senior facilities professional is in tune with the vision of the organisation.

As the organisation evolves over time the strategic direction may need to be modified to take account of external influencing factors, which will require an emergent strategy to be developed – this approach may also mean that elements of strategy remain unrealised (see Figure 1.1).

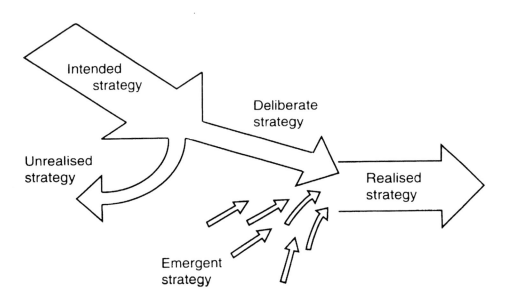

Figure 1.1 Modification of strategic direction over time.

Adapted from Barrett (1995: 55).

20

The developed FM strategy must, however, take account of the core business of the organisation and its own corporate strategy, direction, mission and values. If facilities are to develop in harmony with and at the same pace as the organisation that it supports then it must develop a degree of strategic alignment and focus upon shared values, but also and perhaps more importantly the facilities manager must become a part of the decision-making body (i.e. a board-level player) if facilities are truly to become proactive.

The strategic dimension

Research carried out by Sheffield Hallam University (Rees, 1988) which looked at FM structures within the NHS has shown that the percentage of directors of facilities management working for NHS trusts who were executive directors on their trust boards rose from 10% in 1995 to 24% in 1997. This would indicate an increasing awareness of the significant role that the profession can have in the NHS. In this context comparisons with local government (FMGC unpublished reports) indicate that the NHS became aware of the benefits that can be obtained from the development of departments of facilities management ahead of other UK public sectors in the UK.

The Sheffield research highlights the move of facilities issues from the boiler room or kitchen to the boardroom as more and more organisations realise the true potential of managing the facilities portfolio in a strategic manner. With this in mind facilities professionals must train and develop themselves (board-level grooming). This will require facilities managers or directors to learn to speak the language of the board (balance sheets and business cases as opposed to inches, formulae and kWhs). It is estimated that traditionally in most NHS trusts the size of the facilities budget comes second only to staffing and wage costs. On average facilities budgets represent approximately *20%* of the overall budget of the host organisation – a statistic which should serve to reinforce the need to develop effective and innovative strategies to ensure that facilities services are delivered in a manner which demonstrates value for money.

Pointers to develop an FM strategy

- Draw a line in the sand – where are you now? *Scope the current service provision. Establish user perception on the range of services provided under the facilities banner.*

- Business process re-engineering. *Ask: Why do we do the things we do? Do we need to do them? How could we do them better? What else do we need to do?*

- How are services currently provided and how is it anticipated that these services will be provided in the future? *Are there any pointers in the organisational strategy? Will services be provided in-house or outsourced? If outsourced will services be provided as single service contracts or contract bundles/TFM (total facilities management)?*

- Identify shared values with the host organisation. *What are the aims of the organisation? Has it got a mission or vision statement? If so can the facilities mission/vision statement be aligned with it to set common goals or values? What facilities standard does the organisation want/expect?*

- What are the short-, medium- and long-term service objectives of the organisation? and for facilities? *Where will the organisation be in 5/10 years? What markets will it be operating in? How will facilities need to adapt or change to support this future view? These may need to be listed on a service-by-service basis. Identify a range of short/medium and long-term objectives for the directorate at a corporate level and for individual service functions such as catering, security domestic services, etc.*

- What are the 'knowns' and what are the unknowns with respect to the future? *What has been clearly stated with respect to strategy and development? What might cause that strategy to change – new technology, new materials, etc.?*

- How will the strategies be reviewed/realigned to take account of emergent strategy? *Set review goals– short-term goals to be completed within 12 months medium-term within two to three years with a review after year one. How can 'real time' influence be tailored into emergent strategy?*

Where possible link strategic objectives to the achievement of known standards for specific functions of service provision such as the Charter Mark Award for government or public services, ISO 9002 or similar quality standard, secured by design secured car parks accreditation (Association of Chief Police Officers) or Gold Award car park standard for secure car parks, etc.

Specific service objectives will need to be established for the portfolio of FM services provided. The pace of development outlined will to some extent be determined by the point from which you start. For example, the strategic objectives for Security could be:

Short term

- Review provision of security services.

- Upgrade CCTV to main entrances and car parks.

- Provide 'personal safety and awareness training' to key staff.

- Undertake security audits to establish objectives which will demonstrate improvements to on-site security.

- Develop violence and aggression training for front of house staff.

- Review/produce a security strategy and security policy.

- Develop benchmarking information.

Medium term

- Achieve improved car park security.

- Review security strategy.

- Conduct a feasibility test on the corporate access system.

Long term

- Review security requirements on site.

- Review CCTV monitoring arrangements.

- Tender/re-tender the security service.

The above list is fairly generic to most sites and the content could be varied to suit , depending on the state of the service or the availability of policy/procedure at the time of developing the strategy. When developing individual strategies and procedures the development or implementation of proposals can be mapped or planned to take effect over the period of the short/medium/long-term objectives. Obviously the medium-term plan must allow for the service in part or in total to be reviewed to take account of internal changes within the organisation or external pressures that emerge, e.g. a change in statutory standards that will need to be complied with. Some of the objectives may directly improve the service while others may improve access to the service or open the service out to a wider audience – again it is important to establish the strategic direction and values of the organisation to ensure that the FM services are developed in an effective and supportive manner.

Obviously some factors such as a change in statutory compliance requirements will act as drivers and will force strategic priority to be reconsidered. Other drivers could be driven – perhaps at a different pace – to adopt best practice or to examine information gained from benchmarking etc. The point here is that once a strategy has been developed and objectives set it does not mean that a blinkered view must be taken or that the strategy must be rigidly adhered to – the trick that most successful organisations have found in order to be successful is to reinvent themselves before the service peaks, that is to take into account the internal and external change drivers, anticipate the market and potential internal/external influencing factors and to reposition themselves to deal with future scenarios.

Figure 1.2 shows that as an organisation reaches point A on the development curve it must reconsider the way it operates and the markets that it operates in. It must reinvent itself in order to position itself to take on new and challenging markets and to grow. Reinventing the organisation, if carried out correctly, should avoid the organisation reaching position B on the curve which represents the end of its useful and economic life – when systems/procedures and product popularity is declining and the organisation's market share is being overtaken by competitors. By the time a company reaches position B it is often too late to save the it – as it has failed to recognise the need to make any change (in systems, processes, markets, information technology, etc.).

THE FACILITIES MANAGER AS THE CHANGE DRIVER

The provision of facilities management is by its very nature dynamic and constantly changing to support the needs of the organisation. The factors which influence and ultimately drive change within organisations are quite neatly encapsulated in the 3 Ps model of facilities management constructed by DEGW (see Figure 1.3).

Business Survival
Sigmoid Curve

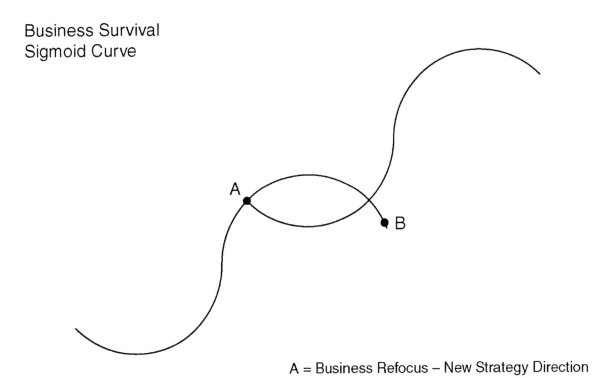

A = Business Refocus – New Strategy Direction

B = Business Failure

Figure 1.2 Handy business sigmoid curve.

(*Source*: Handy, 1994: 50.)

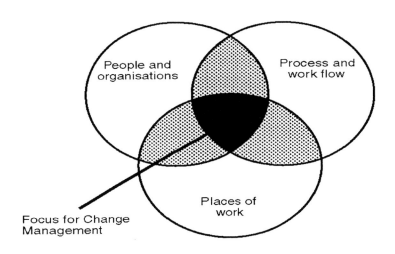

People and organisations

Process and work flow

Places of work

Focus for Change Management

Figure 1.3 DEGW's 3 Ps model.

The model identifies the interface points between the 3 Ps and illustrates the impact that a change in environment or place of work can have upon the process and workflows that take place within the built environment and the knock-on impact that this can have upon people and the organisation. For example, if a multi-site manufacturing company consolidated its activities onto one new, large site, the process and workflow activities/systems would change as a result of the move, and there is a good chance that in a new and purpose-built hi-tech factory a smaller, more efficient workforce utilising up-to-date technology would be in operation. At the centre of the three circles is the area that highlights the focus for facilities management – the opportunity for the facilities manager to become the change manager and to become more proactive rather than purely responsive. Who better to co-ordinate all of this change/churn which has an impact on all of the key areas outlined in the definition of FM given in the introduction? Some may disagree with the facilities manager being put forward as a change manager, but who else is best placed within the organisation? The facilities manager often is in a better position than other board members to co-ordinate the various elements of change.

Whilst change is all too often the result of other influences, if the facilities manager is a board-level player who is, in turn, tuned into the future direction and needs of the organisation, then the FM should be regarded as the change manager, alert to the interaction that occurs between property, people and the organisation. If the FM can achieve this role then he or she is truly a strategic operator, able to contribute to discussions relating to property procurement, space utilisation and workflow/process within the building envelope which will impact upon future work scenarios. The FM department must become more strategic and have the foresight to anticipate and predict change and retain or develop the flexibility to adapt to it. This focus for change management presents the facilities manager with the opportunity to co-ordinate and package the required portfolio of goods and services that best supports the needs of the organisation. The facilities manager must also be alert to those changes within the profession and within the host organisation's market sector that are relevant and will be of benefit to the company's core business.

ORGANISATIONAL SYNERGY

Earlier in this chapter the importance of shared values was highlighted. In terms of strategy the facilities manager must be able to demonstrate that the services that he or she provides add value and not cost to the service supply chain. The FM must ensure that the services that are provided dovetail into the overall service delivery in a supportive and seamless manner. In this respect it is essential that the facilities strategy and the values that are shared are monitored and reviewed in 'real time' to ensure that facilities are in tune with the organisation and that they are both travelling in the same direction. Real-time scoping is important but it needs to be guided with one eye on the horizon (which is often shifting) to anticipate future directions and the other eye trained on possible external influences that could alter strategy (such as new technology or social/economic trends).

RE-ENGINEERING

Once the line in the sand has been drawn with regard to how services are currently being provided and a view has been established regarding how services should be provided, the next step in the process is to question everything!

- Why do we do the things that we do?

- How do we do them?

- Do we need to do them?

- How could we do them better/more efficiently?

All too often working practices and procedures can become entrenched, inflexible and inappropriate, and remain unquestioned. Often the view 'we have always done it like this' is stated and when a service provider becomes too close to an issue it can be difficult to step back and view it in a different way. People often feel comfortable with what they know and see change as a threat.

The re-engineering of processes and work patterns can be stressful and difficult to achieve, and is often seen as an attempt to downsize the organisation. For re-engineering to work it must be supported at board level and must therefore be a top-down and bottom-up initiative. Hammer and Champy (1995: 6) detail the key players who should form part of the re-engineering team and also outline some of the difficulties of the re-engineering process. Often change can cause resentment in the workforce, particularly during the mobilisation of contracts that follow on from market testing exercises which have resulted in the in-house team being transferred to the new service provider under the TUPE arrangements (i.e. the provisions of the Transfer of Undertakings (Protection of Employment) Regulations 1981). The amount of time required to manage the change associated with such a transition should not be underestimated (considerable time and effort will be required from the HR department) and the mobilisation phase of the contract needs careful planning as it is not unheard of for aggrieved employees to sabotage the process. However, on a positive note the author has experienced situations where in-house teams, demoralised due to lack of support or funding and labelled as poor performers, have been transferred over to contractor service providers following a market test. The resulting change in work output and individual performance and attitude has been incredible – the same staff but motivated in a different way. Staff who once claimed 'we have always done it this way – this is only way it can be done' suddenly become champions for the contractor, clearly enjoying the opportunity to be innovative with respect to the tasks that they previously carried out in perhaps restricted ways that had remained unchallenged/unquestioned for years. Thus change may be brought about simply by involving those that carry out the tasks and listening, evaluating and acting upon their views.

Figure 1.4 shows Hammer and Champy's 'business system diamond' (Hammer and Champy, 1995: 4) and illustrates the changes that occur when a business (in this example the facilities business unit) re-engineers its processes. All aspects of the service provision will be altered in some way as a direct result. People, jobs, management and organisational values are all linked together.

- The top part of the diamond represents the business processes or the way work is done in the organisation, and this will determine or influence the personal profile or performance criteria of an employee/group of employees or facilities contractors in support of those business processes (relating to jobs and structures).

- Employees or contractors are performance measured or monitored and ultimately they are paid in relation to their performance against set criteria, specifications/standards or management measurement systems. These measurement systems will in turn serve to shape the values, culture and beliefs held by the employee or contractor. (For example, with regard to culture, if the measurement systems are orientated around measuring customer satisfaction, then the adopted or developed culture will be to delight the customer or to provide excellent customer service. Alternatively, if the systems are set up to monitor against specification in an adversarial fashion then the adversarial stance will be adopted by both parties resulting in a loss of goodwill).

- The values and beliefs will shape the business processes. (For example, they may be designed to satisfy the customer or to play exactly to specification – in the latter case stifling innovation.) This modified organisational culture then supports the business processes.

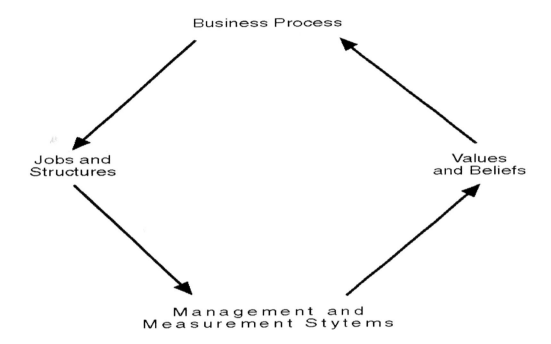

Figure 1.4 Hammer and Champy's business system diamond.

(*Source*: Hammer and Champy, 1995:4.)

STRATEGIC OUTSOURCING

An effective way of adding value to the facilities service provision is to package the services in order to give best effect, maximise flexibility and gain economies of scale. Charles Handy (1994: 26) wrote:

> Organisations are responding to the challenge of efficiency by exporting unproductive work and people as fast as they can.

This shift towards outsourcing has been widespread particularly in local authorities and the NHS – outsourcing, downsizing, delayering and contracting out are all terms that have been used to describe the process of exporting workload and staff groups out of the organisation. It is fair to say that in the early waves of market testing and compulsory competitive tendering, on the whole many organisations were not well prepared to go to the market. For some, competitive tendering was compulsory and a relatively new process. Often specifications were poorly prepared and incomplete resulting in post-contract variations, or alternatively so detailed and complex that contractors were scared off or bid high in order to offset or cover the risks. Suffice it to say both purchasers and providers got their fingers burned. Often decisions were taken to market test for all the wrong reasons – in some instances hidden agendas or the inability to manage or change inflexible, difficult or outdated groups of staff were the hidden drivers to go to the market in order to 'outsource' problems that should have been managed in-house

Absolute clarity is required with respect to 'how services are to be provided in the future (the package) and who will provide them (in-house or contractor).' Clearly a more strategic view is required with respect to outsourcing the range of FM services which have previously been described as vital enabling functions. The facilities strategy must contain a considered and detailed view of the most appropriate portfolio or make-up of the facilities package that is to be put to the market. Every opportunity must be explored to ensure that the package is attractive enough to invite sufficient competitive interest from contract suppliers yet is constructed to maximise the potential that can be gained from economies of scale whilst delivering services over a stated period. In some instances a balance must be struck between what's right for the organisation (specification/standards) and what is attractive for the market (contract bundling to achieve generic working or economy of scale). A crucial part of the initial facilities scoping exercise is to establish a timetable of FM contracts that are currently in place, so that a view can be taken with respect to co-ordinating the most attractive package with which to go to the market. It may be worth considering extending some existing contracts in the short term to enable contracts to terminate at the same time to give the best package whilst avoiding potentially expensive and disruptive contract buy-out situations.

Another key consideration with respect to contract bundling and facilities strategy is contract duration. If the market is to continue to mature, risks will need to be taken with respect to extending the duration of facilities contracts. Both sides incur considerable expense when testing the market and the process can be extremely disruptive. Contractors want longevity of tenure and to avoid the expense and associated aggravation involved in retaining the contract in a market test. Three-year contracts are simply not long enough to allow shared values or true benefits to be realised. There needs to be a commitment to enter into longer contracts (7–10 years) with clear goals and contract milestones mapped for the life of the contract. Private Finance Initiative (PFI) schemes are currently being signed to cover the provision of facilities services for periods of 25 or 30 years (structured as part of BOOT – build, own, operate and transfer – of DBFO – design, build, finance and operate – schemes) although market test options are often written in at five-yearly intervals. It will be interesting to see how these schemes develop with respect to performance, cost and post occupancy evaluation. In these schemes the consortia involve the facilities provider at an early stage in the design in order to establish any operational difficulties associated with the it. In this way maintenance and operational problems may be designed out at the beginning and so both the consortium and the facilities operator will not have to endure such problems over the life of the building/contract. (PFI is discussed in more detail later in this chapter.)

It is vital that the package of services is constructed to complement the facilities strategy and that there is clarity behind the decision to market test as there are advantages and disadvantages to testing the market:

Market testing advantages

- Clear standards and improved quality of services (due to focus on performance outputs).

- Innovative bids received from in-house and external providers.

- Emphasis on monitoring of contracts and service level agreements, leading to an increase in efficiency and effectiveness.

- 100% focus can be provided by specialist contractors in the field of catering etc.

Market testing disadvantages

- Not always a successful exercise – in some instances costs can soar.

- Contracted services can fail to meet or maintain quality standards.

- Once a service team has been outsourced it is costly and difficult to bring a team back 'in-house' as the knowledge and training (often a valuable but unquantifiable resource) is also outsourced along with the particular service.

THE EUROPEAN PROCUREMENT PROCESS FOR GOODS AND SERVICES (PUBLIC BODIES)

Public procurement law states that any public service contract with a sum total in excess of the relevant threshold must comply with EU/GATT legislation when going out to the market to test services. Compliance with the directive is mandatory. The purpose of the directive is to promote and maintain competition in public procurement within the European Union, to control restrictive practices and to try to create a level playing field for potential contractors competing for work. There are three procedural options:

- restricted;

- open;

- negotiated.

The restricted procedure is the most frequently used within the NHS and enables the selection of tenderers to be controlled. The contracting authority invites interested parties to show an expression of interest and from the received expressions a selected group are invited to tender.

The open procedure is also available but is less frequently used as it allows all of those expressing an interest to receive tenders and has a longer period (52 days) for receipt of expressions of interest.

The negotiated procedure requires careful consideration as it attracts ministerial attention. There needs to be clear reasons why the negotiated route has been chosen over the open and restricted options and it is only available in limited circumstances.

All contracts exceeding the following totals with effect from 1/1/2000 to 31/12/2001 (ex VAT) must be advertised in the *Official Journal of the European Community (OJEC)*:

- Supplies   £93,896

- Services   £93,896

- Works   £3,611,395

The advertisement in the *OJEC* must be placed for a period of 37 days prior to the invitation to tender. Tenders have to be issued for a period of not less than 40 days to those responding to ITT (invitation to tender). Within 48 days of a contract award notification must be placed in the *OJEC*. Selection of tenderers from those responding to the advertisement must not discriminate on grounds of nationality etc. Criteria for exclusion are very specific and must be capable of full justification to demonstrate fairness of the selection process to all of those responding to the advertisement.

Exemptions to the procedures

Bearing in mind the purpose of the legislation, exemptions are limited and are strictly defined. In the case of genuine urgency (failure to plan ahead is specifically excluded) an accelerated procedure may be allowed – an example might be the sudden and unforeseeable failure of a critical piece of equipment, but not the sudden and unexpected release of funds which may require fast-track procurement in order to spend/commit funding before the financial year end. Lack of financial planning does not constitute an emergency.

Where appropriate, therefore, the period for receipt of expressions of interest may be reduced to 15 days and the tender period to 10 days.

Implications of non-compliance

Where suppliers feel that they have been unfairly disadvantaged they are encouraged to seek redress through he Compliance Directive. Therefore in any circumstances where a supplier is excluded from competition the reasons must be set down and must be applied equally to all suppliers.

Statistics and monitoring

The government requires an annual return from all public bodies showing the value of business placed within and outside of the directives. Failure to comply with the legislation is unlikely to go unnoticed.

Below is a list arranged is sequential order detailing the elements that are to be considered and actioned when entering into a public body market testing or outsourcing project. The elements could equally be used or modified for a range of service procurement exercises and the elements are not exclusively relevant to public body market testing.

Checklist for market testing

- Prepare draft timetable mapping the whole process.

- Prepare and place *OJEC* advert (public bodies) or advertisement requesting expressions of interest.

- Prepare conditions of tender and draft conditions of contract.

- Prepare and approve the service specification.

- Receive expressions of interest.

- Select the companies that will be invited to tender.

- Send out tender documents with a covering letter.

- Write to any unsuccessful companies.

- Arrange and attend tenderers briefing meeting.

- Receive tender submissions.

- Undertake analysis of submissions and draw up shortlist.

- Write to shortlisted companies inviting them for interview.

- Write to unsuccessful companies.

- Attend interviews.

- Select the successful tenderer.

- Write to the successful company.

- Write to unsuccessful companies.

- Prepare and place *OJEC* award notice (public bodies).

- Agree mobilisation process.

- Prepare and issue final contract for the contractor and the organisation to sign.

PARTNERING

Partnering is not a new concept within the construction industry – a report published in 1994, *Constructing the Team* by Sir Michael Latham, recommended partnering as a way forward to avoid adversarial contract relationships. There is some evidence that partnering can work – particularly in the construction industry with high-profile companies partnered with large construction companies (Sainsbury's plc). The results of some American research on partnering is set out in *Partnering – Contracting Without Conflict*, a National Economic Development Office publication (NEDC, 1991). The NEDC definition of partnering is as follows:

> A long term commitment between two or more organisations for the purpose of achieving specific business objectives by maximising the effectiveness of each participant's resources. The relationship is based on trust, dedication to common goals and an understanding of each other's individual expectations and values. Expected benefits include improved efficiency and cost effectiveness, increased opportunity for innovation and continuous improvement of quality products and services.

It is important to stress that partnering is different to a partnership. In its simplest form a partnering agreement is no more than a charter which is neither legally nor contractually binding whereas a partnership implies joint venture with shared profits. Partnering is all about shared vision, innovation and improved service delivery. There is also a difference between project partnering (an agreement specific to a one-off project) and strategic partnering which could cover a number of projects over a number of years.

Some large and well-known construction firms have worked with established teams of contractors and subcontractors on a number of large projects and there are now a growing number of national retail companies that have successfully partnered with contractors for the construction and upgrade of retail premises. In some cases these partnering arrangements have been operating for a number of years. This has given benefits to both parties.

Client benefits

The client is familiar with the efficiency, working practices/procedures and quality of work and can mobilise new projects with reduced lead in times. A standard design approach can be utilised enabling a fast track from design to construction which results in reduced project costs. Costings can be linked to a schedule of rates (both partners having experience of cost and performance from their previous projects together). The client can also avoid the expense and delay of tendering each project and working with a new set of unknowns (architects, consultants, builders, building services engineers, etc.) on each project. This also serves to reduce the 'claims focused culture' which results in litigation and dispute that can often result from specification variations and delay, all of which will have a significant impact on the total scheme costs.

Contractor benefits

For the contractor there is a body of work that allows a degree of employment security (enabling teams to develop and work together and allowing the development of contractor/subcontractor relationships). It usual for a partnering arrangement to be set up to cover a number of projects as the initial costs of the partnering approach can be higher than the traditional contract procurement methods. Contractors will enjoy the benefit of establishing regular payment mechanisms and economies of scale for procurement. Generic operating and services manuals can also be produced with core elements and design philosophies/building services specifications etc. relevant to each project. A reduced construction phase is often realised as a result. The contract partner has the prestige of being linked in a partnering arrangement with the client (who may have a high profile). The contractor also has more influence on the design process.

There is also evidence that a partnering approach can have significant benefits in supply chain management. Many organisations recognise the importance of their suppliers and provide support and nurture, particularly those who operate a 'just in time approach to supplies and storage (e.g. car manufacturers and their component companies). In some instances, however, subcontractors are not treated as partners in the process but are often squeezed on price and subject to payment delays.

The concept of facilities management partnering follows the principles of the seamless or 'virtual' organisation which is introduced in Chapter 4, and is reliant on having shared values, a common agenda/vision and trust. Partnering with respect to facilities management service delivery is a frequently discussed concept but to date is seldom achieved in reality. Many within the FM industry agree that partnering is the way forward for facilities contracting – and it does represent a move away from the traditional adversarial approach to contract service delivery. This approach offers the opportunity to embrace innovation and share risk, but for now the concept is still in its infancy in the facilities arena (though there are champions coming through within the FM field). There are a number of contractor organisations that claim to be partnered with their FM provider but all too often partnering in the true sense of the word is not followed through. For it to be a true partnering arrangement then there must be an element of risk and reward for both parties – a move away from the view that 'when things are going well you are my partner' and 'when things are going badly you are my contractor'. Clearly partnering in FM will be an initiative to watch in the coming years.

THE PRIVATE FINANCE INITIATIVE (PFI)

In November 1993 Kenneth Clarke (then Chancellor of the Exchequer) described PFI as 'a radical and far reaching change in capital investment in public services'. Private financing for public schemes was widely hailed as the way forward for the cash-strapped public purse and a move away from the view that publicly funded capital projects and new builds were not well managed which often resulted in:

- time overruns on projects;

- cost overruns/cost escalation;

- over-engineered designs.

The Treasury report *Setting New Standards – A Strategy for Government Procurement* analysed a total of 803 public projects in 1993/94. The results showed that:

- 6.5% of the projects took longer to complete than originally forecast;

- on average the projects cost over 13.1% more than the initial budget allocation.

PFI has to date been used as a vehicle to fund a wide range of high-profile and varied projects such as the Channel Tunnel rail link, prisons, hospitals, fire stations, roads and bridges.

The thrust behind PFI is to transfer risk to the private sector (risk of construction, risk of financing and risk of operation). Construction risk is generally easier to identify and quantify than operating risk. The procurement process for PFI is long and detailed as any expenditure by the public sector must demonstrate 'Value for Money'. Value for money is demonstrated through the efficient use of assets, a lifecycle approach to maintenance and utilising the focus, expertise and capital that exists within the private sector – in short the transfer of risk from the public to private sector has to be demonstrated. A Public Sector Comparator (PSC) or reference project has to be completed which in essence is a benchmarking exercise to establish what the scheme would cost if it were to be constructed using capital from the public purse.

PFI bidders form a consortium that includes financial backers, lawyers, facilities operators and constructors – the complete team required to design, build and operate the building. A recent change to PFI guidance has stated that the inclusion of soft FM (catering, cleaning, security, etc.) is now optional – however, the inclusion of these soft FM elements are often the additions that can make the scheme more attractive to the market. The consortium is often set up as a limited company or a limited partnership and the public sector then pays the consortium for the building and the operation of a range of agreed services provided within it as part of the PFI package. This is achieved by means of a unitary payment mechanism which covers the financing costs and the service/operational costs for the term of the contract. Payment consists of both fixed availability payments relating to the physical building and the desired working environment and service related payments for the package of FM and operational services. Monitoring is required to check availability and this monitoring is often facilitated using an FM helpdesk (see Chapter 5). Non-availability of a room due to a water leak, electrical failure, etc. results in a penalty for the consortium. Both the consortium and the public sector management team will have monitoring teams to log this availability and service quality data.

The financing of PFI projects can be for periods of 25–30 years and public sector comparators and investment appraisals have to be carried out in order to establish the feasibility of the PFI proposal. The early PFI feasibility exercises led to abortive work and high bidding costs which wasted both time and money and this slowed the market, with consortia being very selective regarding the schemes they bid for. PFI is still in its growth phase and has yet to reach maturity. However, the new Labour government has reviewed the lengthy process required to get a PFI project off the ground and the next few years should see more schemes being delivered and more projects being procured through the scheme – allowing more public funds to be redirected to other areas of pressure.

From a facilities perspective PFI will undoubtedly have an effect on contracting. PFI will force the partnering agenda as consortia position themselves to win business that has to be sustainable operationally over contract periods which will be longer in duration than the traditional 3–5 year term. The public sector must consider the range of FM services that are to be included as part of any PFI project as the FM package may be the deciding factor that makes the project look attractive enough for the private sector to make a bid. FM services will constitute a large part of the costs for the operational life of the building, e.g. an £80 million new build project with operational service costs of £5 million per year provided by the consortium for a period of 30 years will represent a PFI deal that has an operational bias considering the ratio of capital costs to operational costs over the life of the contract. This demonstrates the importance of constructing the right FM package – particularly when the PFI project is a new build block on an existing site. Consideration must be given to including the other existing on-site FM services in with the PFI package in order to attract economy of scale (e.g. only one set of overheads etc.). This may be attractive in order to tackle backlog maintenance issues and to avoid having a two-tier service standard on site (one standard for the PFI building and another for the existing estate). Cost modelling linked to benchmarking will aid the decision. It will be interesting to monitor the effect that PFI has on partnering as this concept will link the designers, construction team and the FM operators along with financial backers in a consortium team that will effectively design, build, finance and operate the building (DBFO). This approach links the operators with the designers and enables the operators to influence the design so as to avoid maintenance and logistical problems and ensure that the building functions operationally as intended. All too often the design team and the builders build the building and then move on to the next project – leaving the operators to deal with the issues that develop from using the building and post occupancy evaluation. With PFI, if the consortium gets it wrong, then the high maintenance costs and increased operating costs associated with running an inefficient building will sit with the consortium – resulting in possible financial penalties. As PFI contract agreements may well be for a 25–30 year term the design and operation needs to be thought through very carefully. In some PFI deals the FM operators may also have some limited financial equity tied up in the deal – in which case the risk and reward concept comes into play

This first chapter has outlined the importance of developing a facilities strategy. This strategic theme will form a common thread throughout this publication and will link into the other chapters.

CHAPTER 2

Customer Focus

This chapter will concentrate on the principles of customer focus and the concept of providing a 'seamless' one-stop shop for facilities services which will ensure that facilities services are accessible and appropriate and can serve the requirements of both the host organisation and the customer. However, to do this is it is vital initially to identify:

Who the customer is.

The chapter will highlight the difficulties that can be encountered when applying established organisational and management theory into practice in a practical or work-based setting. Areas of conflict will be highlighted in relation to user needs vs. organisational needs (i.e. micro vs. macro issues). The importance of effective and relevant service specifications will be reinforced, demonstrating that the service specification forms the blueprint of effective service delivery and that specifications can be either input or output based. If the specification is the blueprint for service delivery then service level agreements are vital to underpin the construction of solid and reliable service delivery. Statistics show that there are real benefits in developing an effective service recovery strategy for the instances when service delivery goes wrong, that is effective corrective action applied 'right time – first time'.

SPECIFICATION

Many of the advantages and disadvantages outlined in the section on market testing (see Chapter 1) are directly related to the quality of the service specification. The specification is the blueprint for the contract (the route map to effective service delivery) and as such only comes second to the FM strategy with respect to key facilities documentation. Clarity of specification is vital and the level of detail and the incentive for service providers to provide innovative approaches and solutions to facilities problems can often be determined by the choice of adopting an input or an output specification approach. The specification represents the benchmark or standard that the service provider will be measured against (both by the client and by the customer) and as such it is key to the whole process that both client and customer develop the specification or the outline of service requirements jointly. All too often in the past facilities departments have written terrifically detailed specifications which ultimately do not represent services which match the requirements of the customer. Frequently organisations exercise the option to extend the term of the existing facilities contract as it comes up for renewal. Specifications are often 'rolled over' in these instances, without being overhauled or revamped to meet the changing needs of the organisation. In some cases (depending on the quality and content of the existing specification) the service that is delivered does not match the service that was specified. The specification represents a 'snapshot' of a moment in time and is a reflection of the service requirements existing at that time. The dynamic nature of many organisations means that specifications can quickly become outdated and as such ineffective. The customers of FM services need to be consulted and involved at a very early stage in the process to ensure that the facilities department fully understands the needs and the priorities/values of the customer and then build these into the specification. In the past – particularly in the NHS and public sector – there has been a view that the estates or property services department (now facilities) knew best what level and type of service the organisation required and little consultation took place. As a result specifications were often developed in isolation with no dialogue with the users of the service. Was it any wonder then that these services failed to deliver and often resulted in customer dissatisfaction and the service provider being labelled as a poor performer?

The service specification can be developed in many ways and the customer can be involved at all stages of the development process to ensure that the specification is developed from the customer perspective, that is taking into account varying physical environments, conditions and criticalities that may be encountered. For example, in a hospital or healthcare setting effective infection control impacts directly on the length of time a patient spends in post-operative recovery. The specification must therefore reflect the need for effective and stringent cleaning /hygiene controls and may refer to certain industry or professional standards. To take this example one stage further, some departments such as intensive care or operating theatres may have a completely different set of standards, so obviously the service specification needs to be developed to reflect these differing requirements and standards. Generally this level of detailed information can only be obtained from the sharp end or the customers.

The detail required to develop the service specification can be acquired in a variety of ways:

- focus groups;

- questionnaire;

- interview;

- service review.

One point to bear in mind is that facilities management should be done *for* the customer and not done *to* them. If the service specification is not developed from the customer perspective then there is an increased possibility that a difference or gap will exist between customer perception and expectation. These gaps are known as service quality gaps and will be discussed in more detail in Chapter 3. Rust and Oliver (1994: 10) define service quality thus: 'Perceived service quality is a subject matter, service encounter satisfaction results from perceived quality, value performance on non-quality dimensions, relevant prior expectations, and the dis-confirmation of those relevant expectations.' This definition raises a valid point with respect to relevant prior expectations. The whole of the service encounter will be measured against predetermined expectations. There will always be gaps between perception and expectation and it could be argued that developing the specification along with the customer should ensure that these gaps are identified and minimised. The worst thing that a facilities service provider could do is to 'over-promise and under-deliver'. Customers will be satisfied if their expectations are matched and will be delighted if they are exceeded. In general terms customers will be happy if they receive what they expect with regard to results, performance, delivery and behaviour. It is important to consider when evaluating service levels that customers can sometimes learn to live with ineffective service delivery, but when this is discovered (often by a fresh pair of eyes or a new contract manager) the knee-jerk reaction is to implement checks and measures and additional staff to drive up service delivery performance. However, this type of approach can mask the inefficient practices that are inherent in the particular method of service delivery. A service re-engineering approach that questions everything should be adopted. (Monitoring service delivery against service specification will be discussed in detail in Chapter 3.)

In order to identify and close the service quality gaps that may exist between the customer's expectation of the service and the perceived service that is delivered (see the section on Servqual and gap analysis in Chapter 3), an effective feedback loop can be utilised. Figure 2.1 depicts an electronic amplifier feedback loop – feeding part or all of the output back to the input can change the performance of an amplifier. Feedback is added or incorporated with the input in order to enable the required change at the output point. If this description were to be changed from amplifier feedback loop to read facilities or service provider feedback loop the same principles of the electronic feedback circuit could be applied to FM service delivery.

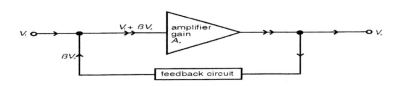

THE FEEDBACK EQUATION

Figure 2.1 Amplifier feedback loop.

(*Source*: Duncan, 1987: 111.)

The input could be represented by the facilities service provision as outlined in the specification, the output being the delivered service. The feedback loop would represent customer demands and the resultant response or the performance monitoring team's efforts in identifying service discrepancy. In essence the delivered service is compared to the stated /specified level of service in order to obtain a level of service balance or satisfaction. If the customer requirement changes then the output requirements are fed back to the input (the specification or SLA) in order to achieve the desired output. This process will be constant and the customer or the monitoring team will drive the speed of the feedback loop. If time is taken at the specification stage to build in customer requirements and demands then the feedback loop would only represent local service variation or service delivery problems. It is essential to focus on the desired outputs and, as circumstances change, the input requirement will need to be altered to support the change.

INPUT vs. OUTPUT SPECIFICATIONS

Input specifications

As discussed earlier in this chapter specifications can differ widely in terms of detail, content and complexity. The use of input-based specifications is appropriate when the range of service objectives or outputs cannot be fully defined, for example:

- breakdown maintenance – considerable uncertainty with respect to spares/consumables and labour requirement);

- security services – majority of tasks will be *ad-hoc*, with each incident tending to be different in many respects;

- *ad hoc* portering duties – intermittent and *ad-hoc* requests for a wide range of services at varying times.

Historic data is used to predict demand in order to identify likely staffing requirements or to match the stated service level. Input specifications are usually quite detailed and outline all of the inputs to the process that the client feels are necessary to provide the service, for example number and grade of staff, frequency of operation, input hours required, supervision per shift, etc. It can therefore be seen that in adopting the input specification approach the roll-over of service delivery can easily become absorbed into the new specification without considering the implications that re-engineering the service delivery may have on tasks, frequency of operation and staffing levels or grades. Input specifications are highly prescriptive and do not allow the service provider room for innovation with respect to service delivery. There can also be a tendency with input specifications to include every imaginable detail with respect to service delivery resulting in a specification which is rarely referred to and which can be offputting to potential providers bidding for the service. Input specifications could be compared to a car insurance policy which is kept in a drawer and only referred to when things go wrong. (On the other hand, however, an adversarial approach to contract management which results in the specification being referred to on a frequent basis is not productive for the client or the contractor.) Because input specifications are so prescriptive, the client has to be careful to ensure that all the necessary detail is included in order to provide the service as required and to avoid post contract variation. This is important because if any requirement is overlooked or missed out at the specification stage then this will result in a variation to the service contract with potential recurrent financial on-costs.

Output specifications

Output specifications could in theory consist of one side of A4 paper stating 'provide a clean facility'. Output specifications should be used when the outputs or the set of service objectives can be clearly defined and demand is predictable:

- collect/deliver 500 items of laundry;

- provide 1,000 meals each day;

- clean and service 12 public toilets.

Clearly more detail would be required (volumes/floor finish etc) together with reference to service standards; industry benchmarks and statutory/professional compliance would need to be included along with information on the facilities and the floor areas to be covered. Different areas or departments may well have different requirements and standards and this would have to be detailed in the output specification Output specifications therefore present the service provider with a framework on which the service can be developed to produce the required and stated outputs. However, some detail on inputs (the 'whats and whens' but not the 'hows') will need to be included in the output specification in order to identify objectives, outcomes, standards, etc. The output specification will set the scene; the service provider then has to construct the service to provide the stated outputs to the required standards. It is at this point that the service provider effectively turns the output specification to an input specification as the inputs (staff, frequency of processes, methods, equipment, etc.) are slotted into place This approach offers some scope and opportunity for the service to be re-engineered and reviewed with respect to innovative approaches to service delivery as the focus is placed clearly on outputs and not how it has traditionally been delivered. This could include generic working or the removal or blurring of demarcation boundaries and complex supervisory structures, working hours, working patterns and procedures.

The evaluation of bids submitted against an output specification can be a problem as a like with like comparison may be difficult. Detailed questions will need to be asked at the bid presentation stage. Monitoring of output-based contracts can also be difficult and often the contractor or service provider will advocate a system of self-monitoring, although this has its own advantages and disadvantages which will be discussed later in this book.

Each organisation will have its own preferences and approach to specification development and the decision to opt for an input or output approach will depend to a great extent upon the criticality of services and the organisational culture. The pros and cons associated with each specification approach are outlined in Tables 2.1 and 2.2 – it is up to each organisation consider which approach is most suitable for them to adopt. One thing is for certain: the specification only represents the starting point for a contract or service level agreement. Performance must be regularly and effectively monitored to ensure that services are delivered to the required standard and specification and that it represents value for money. It is always possible to consider a 'hybrid' approach to specification which seeks to gain the middle ground between input and output specifications – that is which effectively procures the clarity and control of an input specification but which has the potential for innovation of an output specification.

In simple terms:

- input specifications are all about the **how**, e.g. how it should be done, how many staff, how much materials, etc.;

- output specifications focus on the **what**, e.g. what needs to be carried out.

'What gets measured gets done' is a statement that has particular reference to the monitoring of service delivery, and we explore monitoring and performance management further in Chapter 3.

Table 2.1   Pros and cons of specifications based on inputs

Advantages	Disadvantages
Highly prescriptive if well constructed	Time consuming to develop which may put off tenderers or not get fully read. Vital to ensure that all key data is included
Experience of previous service delivery and frequencies can be incorporated	Can stifle innovation – there is a tendency to prescribe how the service is to be delivered.
Consistent format for the tender returns makes evaluation of bids and subsequent monitoring easier.	Can be difficult to evaluate output-based bids while monitoring systems need to reflect the key outputs

Table 2.2 Pros and cons of specifications based on outputs

Advantages	Disadvantages
Relatively concise and straightforward to produce	Client can feel vulnerable if not dictating very clearly the service inputs
Staff can be used more effectively – demarcation boundaries can be broken down to achieve generic working	Difficult to evaluate output-based bids as they will all be different with respect to service delivery
Innovative approaches to service delivery can be embraced	May be short-term staff issues with regard to the 'management of change'

SERVICE LEVEL AGREEMENTS

Service level agreements (SLAs) can be broadly described as 'internal contracts' that are drawn up between the facilities management function and the customers of the FM service. The agreements are often specific to buildings, areas and departments, and if they are drawn up correctly they will outline an agreed level of service that has been defined and developed following discussion between the customer and the facilities department in an effort to best support the local and sometimes unique service requirements of that area. Thomson (1991) states that 'the provision of this type of contract adds a professional edge and avoids the "but I thought you meant ..." syndrome' which is caused by gaps existing between customer perception and expectation of services to be delivered (see the section in Chapter 3 on Servqual and gap analysis). A key aim of the SLA is to avoid misunderstanding and local interpretation. In a hospital, an intensive care department and an operating theatre will have very different and specific service levels and standards compared to an outpatient area because of the problems associated with cross infection through poor hygiene etc. However, some basic specifications that represent 'core' standards/service levels would be the same for most other clinical areas in the hospital and generally these core standards would appear in the majority of SLAs. While the organisation may have a specification which outlines the specific detail for all areas, if the specification were to be broken down to identify the level and frequency of service that each department should receive then this focused data could be used as the measure of service requirement on which to set up a local service level agreement. This approach also pushes the setting of specification data down to the user level which in itself has benefits, for example:

- It promotes self-monitoring – if customers know exactly what, when and how services will be delivered a culture of performance exception reporting is encouraged as they feel ownership of the service levels in their area and are generally keen to let it be known when they do not receive the services to which they have signed up.

- It makes the process of local re-engineering of service levels to suit changed working practices easier and provides scope for re-engineering within the existing contract figure or service allocation.

Breaking down the specification can often serve to eliminate the service gap that could exist if the customer is not fully aware of the range, type and extent of the services on offer (i.e. the service quality gap – see the section on Servqual and gap analysis in Chapter 3). By defining and agreeing the service level it is easier to manage customer expectations with respect to the envisaged service level, which may exceed the available budget. Knowledge of the services that customers should be receiving will also assist in sharp-end monitoring with the informed customer having a sense of ownership relating to the services delivered in their area and often reporting shortfalls and poor performance as they occur.

The SLA should detail the range of services to be delivered to a particular area and also outline the frequencies/timings of the services and the quality standards that the contract delivers against (these could be specific to the functions and activities carried out in that area). SLAs should also detail how service performance and delivery is to be monitored – ideally monitoring sheets should be 'signed off' by a customer representative and offer the opportunity to register any comments that they may have with respect to service delivery. Sharing clear information on performance metrics and monitoring procedures coupled with the detail on the local service specification will help to ensure that the customer does not have unrealistic expectations regarding service delivery and monitoring standards. This in turn will also focus the service provider on delivering to specification or SLA as they will effectively be pushed from both sides

Figure 2.2 depicts the all-embracing contract which is broken down into local SLA packages to aid communication of scope, standards, service delivery and performance monitoring. The FM monitoring team and the customer will monitor the service provision against the agreed SLA, taking up performance and delivery issues with the service provider. A feedback loop is in place to ensure that performance issues or innovation proposals are fed into the FM/customer and if agreed the loop extends to alter the SLA. Performance default is also picked up as part of this feedback loop.

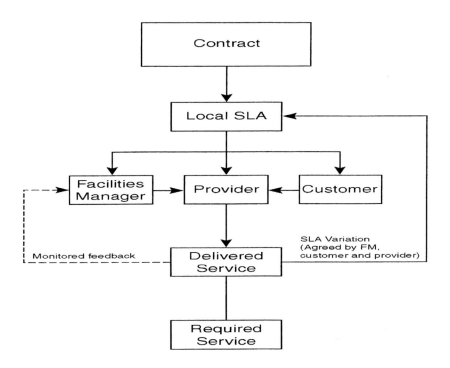

Figure 2.2 Service delivery.

(Source: Payne, 2000.)

Monitoring of service delivery as described in the SLA will from time to time flag up issues or identify trends that may have an effect upon service delivery. The cause of these issues could be that the customer has changed working practices without informing the service provider, or perhaps the service provider has identified an opportunity or innovation which will enable the service to be provided in a different manner resulting in benefits to both parties. In this instance there needs to be effective communications and a robust feedback loop to ensure that service inputs are constantly tuned or adjusted to best suit the customer's required outputs (see the discussion of feedback loops above).

SERVICE CHARTERS

The process outlined above, which links together the overarching specification, the communication of local service standards and frequencies to users of the service, a feedback loop to improve service delivery, a clear and understandable mechanism for performance monitoring and a complaints handling or 'remedy' process, could be articulated into a service charter. Service charters enable the sharing of the specification information which relates to service delivery etc. which all too often is not communicated but kept in the domain of the facilities manager or monitoring team. The use of service charters is on the increase, as highlighted by research carried out by CFM (1999). Service charters need to be regularly reviewed to ensure that they reflect the needs of the customer. The NHS Patients Charter details 'rights and expectations' but because it covers a huge national set-up which has many smaller individual organisations within it, its aims are difficult to achieve and some are remote from discrete organisational aims, objectives and values.

Service level agreements serve to clarify the mystery that often surrounds service delivery with respect to frequency and content of service provision. A well-defined SLA makes the task of monitoring service delivery and proving compliance with the specification much easier.

WHO ARE THE CUSTOMERS OF FM SERVICES?

The argument that the facilities service and specification should be developed from the user customer perspective is ambitious in that it assumes that the service developer or facilities provider is able to clearly identify the customer and is therefore aware of the range and level of complexity of the services required. If a person purchases a loaf of bread from a supermarket then that person becomes a customer. The supermarket, however, has purchased the loaf from a bakery, which makes the supermarket a customer also (already two tiers of customer have been identified) If an FM company were supplying a range of facilities services to the supermarket, who would be the customer for the services provided: the supermarket which directly specifies and purchases the facilities services, or the person who purchases the loaf (defined as the end-user) and who directly and indirectly enjoys the benefits of the services carried out by the FM service provider? Of course the FM provider's loyalty will be with the supermarket as 'whoever pays the piper calls the tune'. In this example it is vital that the services specified by the supermarket are comprehensive and serve to narrow any gaps relating to perception and expectation of standards that may exist between the two customer tiers. For example, the supermarket may focus attention in the FM specification or SLA on equipment availability/reliability with respect to maintenance response to fridges and freezers, etc., perhaps giving this area a high priority rating at the expense of basic fabric maintenance. However, the person buying the loaf may regard the standard and condition of the physical environment or supermarket interior to represent a 'physical marker' or indication of the supermarket's values and culture. In this scenario poor maintenance/decoration could also mean poor hygiene standards etc. in the customer's mind, which may influence the decision to shop there again. The person buying the loaf will 'expect' without question that fridges and freezers will be in working order but he or she may also expect to shop in a pleasant and well maintained environment. If facilities management is to be embraced as part of the total shopping package, or 'supermarket experience' in this example, then in perception terms the front of house will need to be coordinated with behind-the-scenes functionality. (The expectation and perception gaps that may exist between the purchaser (supermarket) and the person buying the loaf (end user) are explored further in the section on 'servicescapes' in Chapter 3.) In a healthcare environment who is the customer of facilities services – the hospital trust, the nurses, the patients, the visitors? They are all customers – each with a different set of values, beliefs, expectations and perceptions, and each requiring facilities support to varying degrees.

Anderson (1993: 177) states 'The customers for health service providers are many. They range from the individual receiving treatment at the micro level, to the health of the local community at the macro level.' This customer or service chain could be likened to the Russian stacking dolls often seen in gift shops – open the outer doll and a smaller doll is revealed inside, and so on and so on. Each doll (or customer tier) is different to the others but all dolls are components that go towards making up the whole. It may be necessary to open three dolls to get to the required doll, and in the same way it may be necessary to service three customer tiers to ultimately service the end user of the system. Indeed, identifying the customer is an extremely complex process. Gronroos (1990: 197) differentiates between the two tiers of customer mentioned above, classifying the person purchasing the loaf as an external customer and the supermarket as the internal customer. The transaction between the supermarket and the bakery could be described as an internal user–server relationship or an internal service function. All service operations contain internal service functions that ultimately ripple through the organisational processes to have an effect upon the 'external customer'. Facilities services ripple through the organisation and impact upon and underpin activity from the top to the bottom of the organisation. Barlow and Moller (1996: 3) detail how the concept of the customer has expanded beyond the boundaries of monetary exchange or payment in kind: 'Customer means not just the paying customer, but anyone who receives the benefit of goods and services, including patients in hospitals, students in schools and public transit riders.'

It is because not all customers are the same that the facilities specification must be developed from the customer perspective. There are no 'off-the-shelf solutions to FM provision – the specification and the service portfolio must be tailored to suit the organisation.

Albrecht and Zemke (1985) developed the customer service triangle (see Figure 2.3). Each point of the triangle represents strategies, systems and people respectively. In the middle of the triangle sits the customer as each activity can be seen in terms of the impact that they have on the customer. Surrounding the customer are the processes, systems, people and interface points that support the customer's needs. This simple framework is a useful tool for visualising the processes and the interdependencies that surround and support the customer. It can be used to identify and map service requirements and assist in developing the specification for those services from the customer perspective.

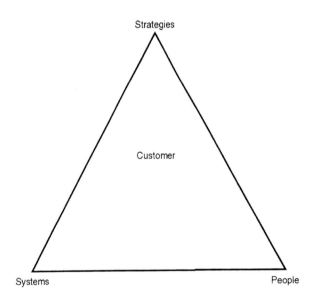

Figure 2.3 The customer service triangle.

(*Source*: Albrecht and Zemke, 1985.)

THE INTANGIBLE NATURE OF SERVICES

Kotler and Bloom (1884: 147) define service as follows: 'A service is any activity of benefit that one party can offer to another that is essentially intangible and does not result in ownership of anything. Its production may or may not be tied to a physical product.' Services are performances, not objects. The service content of a product will have an effect on the customer's expectations; for example, selling timber is almost pure product (tangibles dominant) whereas consultancy work is almost pure service (intangibles dominant). The service environment is quite different to the production environment. In the traditional production environment goods are usually produced in a factory and transported to the customer. Production and consumption are therefore remote from each other, with a buffer (transportation) existing between them. This is not the case in the service environment, where in most instances services are produced and experienced at the point of consumption more or less simultaneously ('the moment of truth' – see below) and without a buffer. It is during this service encounter that the level of service quality becomes apparent and is measured.

Jan Carlzon (1987:3) describes the contact between the front-line staff and customers as 'moments of truth' and suggests that for the time it takes to complete the moment of truth the front-line member of staff *is* the company. He advocates empowerment of these front-line staff, giving them the responsibility for ideas, decisions and actions. Each moment of truth, be it face to face or a telephone conversation, is an opportunity for the reputation of a company to be enhanced or damaged. Customers judge the whole of the company and its behind the scenes operation by the parts which they can see/hear and understand.

Gronroos (1990: 27) suggests that moments of truth may not always be between the customer and the service provider (the customer may not be in attendance) and if this is the case the customer will form a judgement which may be based on the service encounter either before or after the event. For example, if a customer were to take their car into a garage for a routine service, they probably would not interact directly with the mechanic; instead they would probably base their judgement of the service provided on how they were treated in the office while paying for the service or the telephone technique that was experienced while booking the service appointment.

SERVICE RECOVERY STRATEGY

The very nature of the services that facilities providers deliver will attract complaints from time to time (being almost pure service delivery). In manufacturing a 10–12% problem rate is the lowest that some companies can achieve. Diminishing returns may dictate that it is more expensive or difficult to move to a 0–5% problem rate than it is to deal with the consequences of the 10–12% rate. In such cases manufactures will make strategic plans and put systems in place to accept and deal with the complaints that will arise from this anticipated problem rate. The facilities manager must also recognise that there will be complaints periodically and implement an effective strategy for service recovery.

Just because a service provider has considered and developed a service recovery strategy, it should not be seen as a sign that the service provider has decided to provide an imperfect service level. Since all customers are different it will not be possible to satisfy all of the customers all of the time – this is particularly so because service encounters are based upon performance and personal interaction (often influenced by physical and environmental factors and predetermined expectations) and the performance itself will vary from time to time for a number of reasons. Research has shown that 85–95% of customers will do business again if their complaints are resolved immediately and 70% of complaining customers will do business again if the complaint is resolved in their favour. These statistics need to be seriously considered in conjunction the statement that it can cost six times more to attract a new customer than it costs to keep an established one.

The results from the TARP (Technical Assistance Research Programme, Inc.), which details how customer satisfaction is influenced by a company's approach to customer complaints, clearly shows that a good recovery from a complaint leads to the customer's loyalty being maintained at a level similar to that of a first-time perfect delivery of the service. Communication and the swift resolution of problems are key to an effective service recovery strategy. Many organisations operate both verbal and written complaint procedures and have set parameters with respect to processing complaints. A proactive approach from facilities, which ensures that a regular dialogue takes place with all customers, should ensure that planned shutdowns and problems are publicised in advance. *Ad hoc* problems with service delivery etc. cannot always be planned for but again the disruption can be minimised if the extent and likely duration of the problem is communicated to the customers. A truly effective service recovery strategy will have sound contingency plans and 'work-around' arrangements in place to ensure a degree of business continuity. These contingency plans could form part of the organisation's internal disaster plan in which facilities will play a major part.

CHAPTER 3

Facilities Performance and Service Quality

This chapter will look at the benefits of performance monitoring and tools such as benchmarking. The value of space within the organisation will be discussed along with the methodology for conducting a space audit in order to assess if the space that an organisation occupies is efficiently utilised or if there is unlocked potential to 'reshuffle the deck' and use space in a different manner by adopting different work processes and patterns. The latter part of this chapter will concentrate on service quality and how to identify the gaps that may exist between customer perception and expectation.

Facilities services are fairly fluid and because of this a process of constant realignment and performance monitoring is required along with customer feedback to ensure that the service provision mirrors the service requirement. Intangibles are dominant in 'pure service delivery' and tangibles are dominant in 'pure goods'. Goods or tangibles are by and large purchased remote from the provider, often in a retail setting or an environment away from the production area. The intangible nature of services (see Chapter 2), on the other hand, means that the majority of service encounters are conducted 'in the factory' with the provider and the purchaser face to face, that is the service is simultaneously produced and consumed during the 'moment of truth'. This presents a unique set of problems with respect to the monitoring and managing of such 'moments of truth'. The vast majority of service encounters are based upon performance which is largely dependent on the interpersonal skills and training of the service provider at the point of contact. Effective training and empowerment of front-line staff is therefore essential if they are to produce a steady state or constant level of service and feel confident enough to make what they consider to be the right decision when they are required to do so. The concept of the 'servicescape' will reinforce the links between physical and environmental influences and their effect on the outcome of the overall service provision. This concept links intangible elements with tangibles, enabling the service to be developed to take into account the effect of these external influencing factors, or to be tailored to suit a particular environment – to present a feel of the 'total facilities experience' (service wrapping).

MONITORING

Monitoring is a vital process for the facilities manager and should be one of the major tools used to ascertain the performance and quality of service delivery. Regular structured monitoring enables the FM to remain informed about the quality and performance of service delivery while ensuring that the service provider remains focused on performing to specification (that is 'what gets measured gets done'). Following on from a rigorous process to review service delivery or to select the most appropriate service provider following a market test, one of the first activities to be actioned during the mobilisation phase of any new service contract is to set up and agree monitoring systems and procedures. Ideally these systems and procedures will have been considered and developed alongside the service specification prior to tender and evaluation. It is essential that the service provider understands the procedures that will be adopted to measure service delivery performance. This will also highlight the key values and standards that the customer will be expecting and focusing on during the term of the contract on a day-to-day basis. Performance penalty systems must also be agreed up front and signed up to so that both sides are clear about the circumstances that will lead to a penalty variation or deduction from the contract. Even when applying a 'non-adversarial' approach to contracting and service procurement it is advisable to have a performance penalty agreement to provide the leverage to solve protracted performance issues.

The purpose of monitoring is to ensure that a consistent and cost-effective service is provided in accordance with the service specification. To achieve this any monitoring system must be capable of:

- identifying and reporting on the quality of the services being delivered;

- highlighting areas of concern with respect to performance, standards and service delivery against specification or agreed service standards;

- capturing and outlining occasions when a variation to contract is required (following a predetermined process);

- being audited and demonstrating that the delivery of the service is of the desired and agreed quality in order to facilitate payment, variation or performance penalty requests

If managed correctly a structured approach to monitoring which follows clear and agreed procedures and a methodology for quality control inspection and reporting can assist in 'driving up' standards and performance.

Monitoring results or data should be collected and analysed in a way that provides meaningful management information. The following parties can carry out monitoring:

- the in-house monitoring team (internal monitoring);

- an external agency or consultancy (external monitoring);

- the service provider's monitoring team (self-monitoring);

- the end user of the service (the customer).

The in-house team's primary focus is to ensure value for money (to ensure that all that is paid for is received) in accordance with the specification. Where there is no in-house monitoring expertise external monitoring support can be procured on a consultancy basis for specified periods or for independent audit review, although this can often prove to be a costly option. Contractors often promote their ability and desire to utilise self-monitoring on the services that they deliver – but this approach is hardly independent! Cynics would comment that it would always be in the interests of the provider to produce favourable monitoring results. Indeed one aspect of partnering arrangements outlined earlier is self-monitoring. However, in the correct culture and contracting environment self-monitoring can be made to work – after all why pay a contractor to provide a service and then employ an in-house monitor to check that the service is provided? The smart contractor would soon scale down resources in their self-monitoring efforts and use the in-house monitoring results to monitor performance (in fact it may prove cheaper to rectify matters that are picked up this way than to monitor proactively). This would enable savings to be made by the contractor, or hours could be freed up as a result which could be utilised elsewhere in the contract to ease pressure. Following this argument wherever possible use the service provider's data if it has been proved to be accurate and reliable.

During the mobilisation phase of a contract there is a need for internal monitoring and self-monitoring to be carried out by the service provider. This can be beneficial and give a real service delivery focus that can be witnessed by the service provider being monitored. Again, in the right contracting environment, the service delivery should mature to a point where the provider develops shared values with the customer and becomes tuned into the standards expected from them. There should then be consistency between the results produced by the internal and the self-monitoring teams – at this point the need for an in-house monitoring team in the traditional sense should be questioned. On the other hand, if service delivery were variable – perhaps due to adversarial contracting etc. – a structured internal monitoring approach would need to be sustained until such a time that the monitoring results become acceptable and consistent. If the customer is made aware of the service delivery or specified outputs that they should be receiving as part of the service arrangements then customer expectation can be managed. This will also enable the informed customer to recognise when service is not being delivered to specification and to flag this up with the facilities manager. The monitoring team and package of monitoring methods that an organisation adopts will vary according to the size, culture and business of the organisation. Monitoring in some form will be essential and will form part of the input to periodic reviews and service re-engineering. Monitoring tools available to the facilities manager include:

- preplanned routine inspections and follow ups;

- *ad hoc* or on-the-spot inspections;

- agreed rectification periods and penalties for areas that show poor performance (rectification time being weighted according to the criticality of the individual areas being monitored);

- customer or 'end user' monitoring;

- customer interview/focus groups or questionnaires;

- monitoring of customer complaints;

- analysis of tasks and response times logged through the help desk.

A formal approach to monitoring with regular scheduled (weekly and monthly) formal review meetings is desirable in order to achieve and sustain the specified service delivery performance. Consistency is a key word with respect to monitoring and service performance. The monitoring regimes adopted must be consistent in order for a constructive monitor–contractor relationship to be established. Service provider performance must be consistent in order to avoid performance swings which can often occur when contractors firefight or are under-resourced with contract labour (perhaps due to holding vacancies). As the monitoring officer picks up poor performance in one area labour is redeployed from another area resulting in poor performance in that area – and so the spiral of falling standards begins. Peaks and troughs of service delivery are simply not acceptable and this approach fuels the 'what gets measured gets done' mindset. The monitoring team (whoever they are made up from) will need to regularly interface with the users of the service, the providers of the service and the client-side authorised officer. At a predetermined frequency, performance-monitoring information may also be formally reported to the board of directors (a formal monitoring report presentation). Monitoring can be a very useful tool but it needs to be applied in a consistent and even-handed manner in order to develop service delivery in an efficient and flexible manner.

BENCHMARKING

Benchmarking seems to have reached the board-level agenda in most organisations, yet few organisations truly understand the full potential of benchmarking and view it purely as a 'collecting and comparing' exercise, usually motivated by cost considerations. Benchmarking has been defined as:

> The search for industry best practices that lead to superior performance.

> (Camp, 1989)

Benchmarking is all about best practice and improving services by learning from and sharing best practice with others. For many organisations benchmarking is used as an exercise to collect costings and see how they 'measure up' against other similar sized organisations. Often, as long as the figures produced do not indicate that operating costs are high compared to the others in the group, then no further action is taken (this is cost-driven benchmarking). In order to get the true benefit from benchmarking then questions should be asked of the best performers of the group to see how they operate and so establish best-practice methods. If possible and appropriate best practice could then be implemented to improve the service. Therefore comparisons of figures and data should be seen as only the start of the process. Comparisons can be used to group organisations together so that they can then 'get behind the figures' and start to understand the differences in the benchmarking returns. This should lead to a series of questions such as the following:

- What is and isn't included in the benchmark figures (i.e. how were they arrived at)?

- Why do we provide the same service in a different manner and at different costs?

- Are there elements of best practice that can be adopted?

- Can the service be provided to a higher standard at the current cost or to the current standard at a lower cost?

Benchmarking can be conducted internally within the organisation, or externally with other organisations. In the case of healthcare facilities then benchmarking should not be limited strictly to public providers. For example, bed management and admissions could be benchmarked against a hotel chain's bed management operation in order to identify if a hotel (the core business of which relies on the quick turnaround of rooms and room availability and occupancy) has systems and procedures in place that represent best practice which could be incorporated or adapted to improve the hospital services. There are now many benchmarking clubs and consultants offering to carry out benchmarking exercises, but each organisation must carefully consider what, why and how it wants to benchmark, and then deal only with established and competent benchmarking organisations. There is no doubt that benchmarking will mature and become a useful performance monitoring tool that leads to service improvement, but presently the data produced are in the main questionable. Data collection methods allow for a significant degree of local interpretation in the benchmarking returns and as such it is not always possible to accurately or confidently compare 'like with like'. This presents problems as organisations are already making significant business decisions – for example, to outsource – based upon benchmarking data that suggests that the current service provision is more expensive that of other similar organisations. There is danger in this approach!

The public sector is adopting a best value approach to services and procurement and undoubtedly benchmarking will play a great part in this process. Key facilities management performance indicators need to be established along with a clear and consistent methodology for the collection of benchmarking data (i.e. rules and guidelines on what the reported figure should and shouldn't include). For example, the following benchmarks or key performance indicators (KPIs) could be included for facilities services:

Catering

- Pay cost per hour

- Cost per meal

- % food waste

- % customer satisfaction targets met

Portering

- Pay cost per hour

- Non-pay cost per hour

Maintenance

- Cost per m^2

- % response times met

- % PPM to breakdown hours)planned : unplanned)

- Energy cost per m^2

Domestics

- Cleaning cost per m^2 of cleaned area

- % of customer satisfaction standards achieved

- Hours per m^2 of cleaned areas

SPACE MANAGEMENT

Accommodation costs (the costs associated with owning/renting, running and repairing) within a traditional office-based organisation represent the second largest cost to an organisation (staffing being the highest cost). Property costs and the operating costs of an organisation (often expressed as £/m^2) therefore represent a significant proportion of the cost of doing business. Any initiative that can be adopted or implemented to reduce these costs without a detrimental impact upon the organisation will be beneficial. This being so it is vital that the costs of space and the methods adopted to manage space are as efficient as possible. In most organisations the facilities department is ideally placed to control space management issues. The definition of facilities management used in the introduction of this book outlines the role that the facilities manager has with respect to the coordination of people, processes and the workplace.

Often when work practices or processes change additional space is required (or it is perceived to be required) and an extension, a new build or new premises will initially seem to be the only way of accommodating the change. A new build should not be the starting point in solving space problems – that decision should come further down the line and should only be taken when a thorough study into the utilisation of existing space, work processes and work patterns has been conducted. All too often a decision to acquire larger premises is taken prior to considering if the space that is already occupied is utilised in the most efficient manner. The move to larger premises can be costly, disruptive and demoralising, and if this can be avoided by looking at managing space in a different way then this must be a priority. Organisations will evolve to meet the demands of the customer and often this evolution may be sporadic and disjointed. As a result of this evolutionary path many workplace settings have developed in an opportunistic fashion with functions being shoehorned into inappropriate space or accommodation. This can affect production efficiency or operational service delivery. For example, if the goods-in area is situated in the wrong location this could make it necessary to handle materials more than once; likewise, if X-ray is situated on the other side of the site to Accident & Emergency sick patients for routine or emergency investigation will have to be transferred backwards and forwards on trolleys between the two locations along hospital corridors full of visitors.

In an ideal world with a clean-sheet approach to development an organisation would plan the workplace to complement its working practices and workflow/work processes in an efficient and logical manner. For example, the workflow through a production facility would be designed to minimise wasteful handling – with raw materials being input at one end of the process and the finished product output at the other end, avoiding duplication of function and rework items being fed back into the process at a sensible location .In any space utilisation study it is important to map the processes and departmental interactions and linkages in order to work out who frequently interacts with whom, how the workplace operationally fits together and how it is physically provided. The next step is to try to match these linkages in any remodelling exercises that are carried out. Many organisations have developed space standards which may have been developed over a number of years. Space standards will often link function or activity to standard space allocation. Some space standards link to rank or status, while others specify standard room layouts/templates and furniture systems. Space standards will give an indication at the planning stage of the likely spatial requirements for a particular function. Such standards will also assist in the detailed design which combines the functions together in an efficient manner within the building footprint. For example, the NHS has a range of HBNs (building design notes) which contain detailed floor plans and spatial requirements for ward layouts, outpatient areas, etc. – detail which has been developed over time to reflect what works in practice and what does not. Many smaller organisations may not have access to this sort of detail but may have developed their own space standards, perhaps based on hierarchy or status rather than functional requirement, e.g. a manager of a particular grade has a particularly sized office complete with a standard set of furniture to match the grade. Alternatively information is available on space standards in the *Architects' Journal* (*AJ*) technical handbook.

SPACE AUDIT

In order to identify if space is being used efficiently a space utilisation study will be necessary. Space utilisation studies identify how people interact with the physical workplace. They can also identify any spare capacity that exists within the workplace and can point out opportunities for improvement in organisations that perhaps consider they already manage space to optimum efficiency. An effective space audit will take time and will need to refer to accurate floor plans (ideally computer-aided design plans in m^2). In order to establish the true picture of space utilisation data on the use of each room, occupancy numbers and staff working hours will need to be collected from which will follow the progressive linkage of people, processes and workplace. The following definitions can be used to classify or categorise any space or spare capacity within an organisation which has been identified through conducting a space audit:

Standard definitions

Category	Definition
Fixed function space	Company owned space sublet to another party and outside the scope of the space study, i.e. private residents etc.
Specialised space	Specially constructed or serviced areas impractical or costly to modify, i.e. lifts, stairs, plant etc.
Movable function space	Company-owned space within the scope of the space study, i.e. non-specialised ordinary spaces, general-purpose space

Spare capacity– physical use of space

Category	Definition	Cost	Time scale
A	Empty space available immediately	Low	Short
B	Requires changes in work routines or practices to achieve spare capacity	Low/Med.	Short
C	Requires existing function to move to another location to release 'prime space' spare capacity	Med.	Short/Med.
D	Requires building work to unlock spare capacity into historically poorly planned spaces	High	Long

Spare capacity – time use of space

Potential spare capacity expressed as m^2 floor area, based on % utilisation of space within a normal working week of 37.5 hours

Types of space – definitions

- Gross external area (GEA) – area of the whole building around the outer walls.

- Gross internal area (GIA) – area of the whole building to the inside of the outer walls.

- Net internal area (NIA) – gross internal area less all structure and cores.

- Net usable area (NUA) – net usable area less primary circulation.

- Structure and core – walls, columns, plantrooms, stairs and lifts, lobbies and WCs.

- Primary circulation – main corridors and horizontal evacuation routes used for escape in the event of fire.

Using the above approach and definitions a comprehensive assessment of space utilisation can be carried out. The assessment will enable 'what if' scenarios or modelling to take place and if indicative costings are applied to the results for cost/m^2 upgrade, cost /m^2 new build and cost/m^2 revenue costs, then all options and spare capacity identified can be budgeted to aid the decision-making process with regard to using space in a more efficient manner. This will enable budgeting and planning decisions to be more informed. Consideration can also be given to minimising the cost of backlog maintenance, solving departmental or functional problems, to strategically replan function or workflow across the site or to strategically move out of old building stock which may be expensive to maintain and operate into newer accommodation. It is important to note that a space audit represents a 'snapshot' in time of the organisation and as such to be of future use the data will need to be frequently updated to avoid having to start again from scratch at a later date.

One other element that could be considered as part of the space audit would be to identify overcrowding in work areas. Regulations regarding overcrowding are detailed in the Health, Safety and Welfare Regulations 1992 which replaced the Offices, Shops and Railway Premises Act 1963. The Regulations state that a room volume of 11 m^3 per person is the minimum acceptable size for an office. It can be seen from the above definitions that it may be possible to identify spare capacity but to 'free the space up may be uneconomical.

The 24 hours, seven days a week society is now a working reality. Globalisation will also increasingly have an effect on working patterns in order to cover more time zones for trading and on-line or remote support. This change in working practices will perhaps present opportunities in a number of ways relating to space management. For example, it may be possible to fully utilise existing space that is currently redundant or unavailable for long periods of time (e.g. time spare capacity at evenings and weekends, etc.) by offering alternative working patterns or hours to staff (thus providing recruitment and retention benefits) and so on. By sweating the assets in this way an organisation's property will be utilised to its optimum efficiency and such an approach may have a significant effect or impact upon staff travel habits, car use, car parking and commuter traffic. The impact of homeworking and shared space also needs to be explored further with respect to their potential within organisations. Mapping the impact on personnel, on space and on operating costs and organisational efficiency/productivity will enable individual organisations to make choices backed up by hard data and a sound understanding of the benefits and impacts of such an approach. Already by adopting this 'off-site' approach large companies have concluded that they are not in the business of owning property and that property does not enhance the service provided (consider, for example, the property requirements of e-commerce and call centres) or ultimately form part of their core activity.

SERVICE QUALITY AND PERFORMANCE

Zeithaml, Parasuraman and Berry (1985: 41–50) define service quality as 'the extent of discrepancy between customers' expectations or desires and their perceptions'. In other words, the smaller the discrepancy (a close match of both expectation and perception) the higher the level of service quality. Lewis and Booms (1983: 99) define service quality as 'a measure of how well the delivered level of service matches customer expectation'. These two definitions reinforce the fact that service quality measurement is based upon asking customers what their expectations are and their perceptions of the service that they are to receive. However, it can be difficult to link the perceptions that people have regarding a service and the subsequent measurement of that service performance against delivery. Service quality is not measured solely on output or outcome (e.g. how a filling looks after a visit to the dentist) – service delivery will also come into the evaluation criteria (how easy was it to get an appointment, how friendly was the dentist, and so on). Schmenner (1995:18) describes the three attributes of service management that surround a 'moment of truth' or 'service encounter' as:

- *service task* – states why the service exists and what the customer values about the service;

- *service standards* – defines the effective service provision to the customers;

- *service delivery system* – specifies how the service is produced and controlled in terms of cost, quality and customer satisfaction.

Proposing that all three attributes interact to support the service encounter, Senge (1994: 139) warns against focusing on the tangibles relating to service delivery, such as the cost of service and the number of customers served, as this will have the result of 'looking good without being good'. Indeed in some instances the quality of the service can be more important than the price.

SERVICESCAPE AND THE TOTAL SERVICE EXPERIENCE

The concept of the 'servicescape' was developed in an article by Mary Jo Bitner in the *Journal of Marketing* in April 1992. The servicescape is a 'conceptual framework which explores the impact of physical surroundings on the behaviour of both customers and employees. The effects that decor and physical design have on employees and consumers is not a new concept (in the Hawthorne studies (1923–33) the Western Electric Company in Cicero, Illinois in the USA investigated the effects that changing the physical environment, arranging people into smaller work groups and interviewing staff (counselling) all had on productivity). Indeed, supermarkets are now designed to have certain brands and products in strategic locations and at eye level, such as fresh produce and greenery at the entrance to the store, to maximise impulse purchase. The familiar and enticing smell of freshly baked bread is not an indication that the ventilation system is not working – it is another ploy giving out 'buy me' signals to the subconscious mind of the shopper.

While lighting, heating, decor and physical surroundings not only have an effect on levels of productivity and patient recovery in healthcare, they can also have an effect on the outcome of and the ultimate level of satisfaction with the service encounter. Studies have even been conducted into the effect that the presence and tempo of background or 'elevator music' has on service settings, how it influences purchasing and how differing music played at different tempos can appeal to certain age groups. Research has shown that the design and layout of physical environments can influence the resultant responses and behaviour of individuals and servicescapes can be designed to enhance interaction and to complement the type of service encounter that will take place in that location. However, if careful planning can enhance interaction then an inappropriate servicescape can also have a negative effect on the service encounter.

The link between facilities or customer perception and the servicescape concept may be found in the idea that people respond to their environments holistically. 'Individuals perceive discrete stimuli, it is the total configuration or accumulation of stimuli that determines their responses to the environment (Bell, Fisher and Loomis, 1978). This statement reinforces the concept of the 'restaurant experience' whereby customers do not just measure performance of a visit to a restaurant solely on output (how full they were after the meal), they take into account such things as how easy it was to park in the restaurant car park, how friendly the staff were, the restaurant's ambience and décor and the menu choice. This concept could just as easily apply to the hospital experience or the banking experience, etc. The concept of the 'total experience' highlights the links between the tangible and intangible elements within the servicescape. It is these links that could lead to an excellent product being described as merely 'OK' due to the contributing influence of an inappropriate environment or poor service delivery in support of that product.

Caudron (1995: 29) states that 'empowerment programmes tend to fail when management doesn't deal with the environment that influences employee behaviour'. This reinforces the fact that employees as well as customers are affected by inappropriate environmental conditions. It can be seen from the above that facilities services can be developed to cater for varying physical environments and conditions which may have an effect on the overall perception or outcome of the service encounter. Services can be developed with the customer and the environment in mind to provide an element of service wrapping which promotes a total image to suit the unique requirements of and help produce a high level of satisfaction with the overall service encounter.

Sir Colin Marshall, the chairman of British Airways, has extended the 'flight experience' for business travellers to include the flight lounges and check-in procedures in an attempt to minimise the effects that problems with checking in before a flight and recovering luggage after the flight may have on tainting the overall flight experience. Business travel is a lucrative market and every attempt must be made to secure repeat business. Now the flight experience can begin before the traveller actually gets to the airport. This in recognition of the fact that the overall experience is made up of much more than just the flight element – on-line reservation and transport by chauffeur from home to airport are included in the ticket price, thus creating or extending the boundaries of the 'virtual airport'.

ADDED VALUE

Facilities service providers have only one chance to make a first impression on their customers and it is widely accepted throughout the service sector that the initial and hopefully subsequent service encounters are excellent opportunities to add value to the service process. Value added services or added value are regularly used buzzwords within service-based industries.

Seamus Toland (1995) states that value is achieved in facilities management when the facility:

- is wanted/needed;

- is seen as fair value by users;

- meets a defined need;

- meets agreed standards.

The above points are relevant to achieving the most basic level of value from a facility: it has to be required, to meet a need to an agreed standard and be seen as representing fair value. However, customers are becoming increasingly more demanding – customers now expect to recieve added value dimensions to the services that they receive and at no extra cost. They now look for elements of service wrapping or packaging that represent added value and will actively shop around to find it. Zeithaml, Parasuraman and Berry (19) state 'as manufacturing executives find it difficult to establish sustainable technology based competitive advantage, they will direct added attention and resource to value added service – as a truer source of superiority'. Customers want to feel that they are getting more for less or that little bit extra – this is *added value.*

Akhlaghi (1995: 27) details two sets of values. These are values that are essential and are almost taken for granted, and value over and above that which is offered from a competitor:

- *threshold values* – such as hygiene in catering and safety in airlines. These values provide an entry into the marketplace and represent the basic or expected level of service which is to a large extent taken for granted.

- *incremental values* – such as a wider choice of food in catering and better seating in an airline. Incremental values create distinction in the marketplace for the supplier and include an element of added value or an added value dimension.

Following this approach adding value in the facilities management context should be directed at improving the level of incremental values – but not if this results in an inappropriate increase in cost. Carlzon (1987: 24) advocates being 'one percent better at one hundred things instead of being one hundred percent better at one thing'. This approach creates an overall perception of big-picture improvements. If the services that a facilities manager provides form part of the overall value chain and value is added at various stages or links of the chain, then it is reasonable to assume that the value to some extent will ultimately be passed on to the customer. However, each link or internal/external customer will quantify and perceive added value in a different manner in relation to the particular function or activity that they perform.

Peters (1989: 49) describes the five basic value adding strategies as follows:

- Provide top quality as perceived by the customer.

- Provide superior service/emphasise the intangibles.

- Achieve extraordinary responsiveness.

- Be an internationalist.

- Create uniqueness.

By adopting the above strategies (perhaps with the exception of the internationalist strategy which may not be totally relevant in some FM contracts or service provision arrangements) facilities managers can hopefully develop a competitive advantage which is capable of being sustained over a period of time, as long as facilities strategies are revisited or realigned to cater for adjustments in the level of service that the customer wants. If the above strategies were to be adopted when re-engineering and developing the service, considerable value could be added to the process – 'value could be designed or built in'.

SERVQUAL AND GAP ANALYSIS

Servqual is a generic framework that was developed by Zeitaml, Berry and Parasuraman (1985: 41–50) in order to assess service quality in organisations. The assessment is made based upon the expectations and perceptions of the customer. The evaluation criteria for assessing service quality is split into five dimensions:

- *tangibles* – appearance of physical facilities, equipment and communication materials;

- *reliability* – ability to perform the promised service dependably and accurately;

- *responsiveness* – willingness to help customers and provide prompt service;

- *assurance* –knowledge and courtesy of employees and their ability to convey trust and confidence;

- *empathy* – caring, individualised attention the firm provides to its customers.

Zeithaml, Parasuraman and Berry (1985) define service quality as perceived by customers as 'the extent of discrepancy between customer's expectations or desires and their perceptions'. Some definitions of these terms is useful:

expectation – regard as probable; promise of value; prospect of future good.

perception –intuitive judgement; obtain knowledge of through senses; observe; understand.

(Collins English Dictionary, 1988)

The gap between a customer's expectations and perceptions can be simply stated as the difference (or gap) between what the customer thinks they are to receive (expectation) and what they actually receive (perception).

Thomson (1991: 8) uses the following example:

> If you are flying to Glasgow then your need is to get there, but your expectation could be that you expect to arrive within 15 minutes of the quoted arrival time. To win the hearts and minds of customers their expectations must be satisfied.

Expectations are influenced by a number of factors such as:

- *Past experience* of the service will give the customer the impression that they will receive the same level of service next time that they use it (regardless of the fact that the previous experience was good or bad).

- *Word of mouth* – the experiences of friends or family will be brought to the attention of users of the service (a satisfied customer will on average tell five people, whereas a dissatisfied customer will tell on average eleven people).

- *Personal needs* – a customer may expect that the service will be flexible enough to cater for individual or specific needs rather than the service constituting an all-embracing production line process.

- *External communications* – expectations may have been raised by media campaigns or sales staff.

The methodology behind customer assessment of service quality takes into account the overall view of the expected service, considering all influencing factors including the four outlined above. The five consolidated dimensions of service quality (tangibles, reliability, responsiveness, assurance and empathy) are mentally checked off against the customer's pre-formed inventory of expectations and perceptions of the service. The result of this mental stock check or calculation of a number of variables is the customer's view or impression of perceived service quality. This view is formed as a result of a measure of performance or delivery of the various service quality dimensions, balanced against expectations and perceptions.

Donnely et al. (1995: 15–20) state that 'customers typically assess service quality by comparing the service they have actually experienced (the perceived service quality) with the service they desire or expect (their expected service quality). Without adequate information about both expectations and perceptions, the feedback from customer surveys is downright dangerous.' Donnely et al. go on to voice further concerns regarding customer satisfaction surveys which only provide a snapshot of the quality of the services that are being provided. They argue that this type of survey is often seen as a ritual to show stakeholders that the service provider is customer focused and can often lead to inappropriate courses of action or initiatives.

The Servqual conceptual model can be used to identify gaps in the service delivery process by considering the expectations and perceptions of the customer and the key components of the provider's service delivery process. Information for analysis is obtained by means of a structured questionnaire that uses a seven-point scale which ranges from 'strongly agree' to 'strongly disagree'.

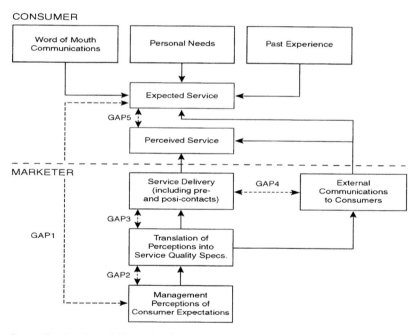

Source: Reprinted from Zeithaml, V.A., Berry, L.L. & Parasuraman, A. (1988): Communication and Control Processes in the Delivery of Service Quality. *Journal of Marketing*, American Marketing Association, April, p. 36.

Figure 3.1 Servqual.

Servqual has been developed to identify five possible gaps in the service delivery process:

- *Gap 1: The Understanding Gap.* This gap is between the customer's expectations and management's perceptions of the customer's expectations. This gap can be narrowed by the provider gaining knowledge of the customer and ensuring appropriate resources, management and communication procedures are in place.

- *Gap 2: The Design Gap.* This gap is between the management's understanding of the customer's expectations and the service quality specification. Gaps that exist here may be due to poor goal setting and inadequate commitment from management to service quality.

- *Gap 3: The Service Delivery Gap.* This gap is between the specification of service quality and the quality of the service that is actually delivered. Gaps in this area can be caused by poor quality control methods, poor staffing and lack of commitment/motivation or resources. Role ambiguity and 'the wrong person in the wrong job' or poor employee job fit will also cause this gap.

- *Gap 4: The Communications Gap.* This is the gap between what has been promised and what is actually delivered in terms of service. Gaps here are caused by over-promising and under-delivering – such promises may have been made in media adverts or in charters such as the NHS Citizens Charter.

- *Gap 5: The Service Quality Gap.* This is the gap between the customer's expectation of the service and the perceived service that is delivered. This is the gap that attracts the most attention and focus.

The use of Servqual to identify gaps such as 1–5 above enables the service provider to locate shortfalls or deficiencies in the services that they provide and also assists in locating where the gaps exist, thus enabling appropriate action to be applied to the required area. The Servqual approach should be utilised at all stages of the development and delivery of service provision. The size, scope and capacity of the customer's requirements will be subject to change over a period of time and if these changes are not identified, either the service provider will end up providing for an increased demand on the service without further resources or the customer may perceive that the overall level of performance has declined, perhaps due to a slower response time caused by the additional workload.

Hiles (1994: 2) states that 'it is all too easy for the service manager to assume that the customer's perception is wrong: it cannot be wrong! It is the customer's perception and will remain so until it is changed.'

CHAPTER FOUR

Flexible Working

This chapter will look at the changing workplace and the potential effect that future working scenarios could have upon the organisation as we currently understand it. The pros cons of homeworking and teleworking will be explored with particular reference to the social, economic and environmental impact that changing how, when and where staff work can have upon the organisation.

FLEXIBLE WORKING

Much has been written, speculated and documented about the advantages and the disadvantages of the changing workplace scenario. 'Work is a thing that you do – not a place that you go to!' The advent of affordable and reliable advanced computer and data technology has enabled staff whose tasks are not dependent on or tied to the workplace to work from home or an alternative workplace. This practice looks set to continue and become more widespread over the coming years. The resultant change in working patterns will undoubtedly offer considerable opportunity and challenge with respect to a range of linked issues, as these new working patterns will affect:

- the organisation – how it is, how it communicates and how it does business;

- communication/control – how does the organisation extend to and support homeworkers?

- social impact – working from home will limit social interaction and could impact upon social exclusion;

- the environment and transport strategy;

- the economy – decentralised business centres, increased Internet and e-mail transactions, the shift of resources from the business community to the local residential community;

- the real estate portfolio and the growing argument 'does the organisation need to own property?';

- the implications of health and safety for 'work' in the home environment.

It is important to note that flexible working is not just about working from home. The concept draws upon the use of a combination of telecommunication and data technology, office systems/furniture, etc. and innovative working practices and routines that enable work to be done away from the traditional centralised, corporate office base. Flexible working requires a totally different approach not only to where work is carried out, but to how it is carried out and organised. 'Spaces are now provided for activities rather than individuals' (Raymond and Cunliffe, 1996: 17). As more staff work from an alternative base, the justification and viability of corporate space will need to be examined in line with organisational strategy and this examination will drive change with respect to new ways of working.

Flexible working – key definitions

- *Annualised/annual hours* – increasingly used in 24-hour organisations such as healthcare and transport. An number of hours for the year are agreed up front (usually the full-time hours). This type of contract enables workload peaks and troughs to be staffed without having to use overtime. Pay is averaged out over the year. Additional hours can be built into the contract to ensure cover for sickness and training.

- *Zero hours (bank staff)* – a flexible contract arrangement favoured by service contractors, enabling workload peaks and troughs to be covered by calling in zero hours or bank staff as and when required. Staff are only paid for the actual hours worked and there is no obligation for the employer to provide work.

- *Portfolio working* – workers are employed by a number or variety of clients (see also Figure 4.1 below). Portfolio working suits team dynamics with teams being assembled to complete projects or tasks of defined duration. Often a portfolio worker is working on a variety or portfolio of contracts/projects at any one time. The downsides are where do loyalties lay, the loss of the company knowledge base, the loss of corporate identity.

- *Telecentre* – an equipped office in a community setting or location, often providing office type facilities (services and equipment) for use by the general public. A range of business services are usually available to provide flexible working solutions to those who lack the space or environment to work effectively from a home base. Equipment can be used on an as and when basis and meeting space or video conferencing facilities can often be hired

THE CASE FOR NEW WAYS OF WORKING

A typical working day for an office building is generally from 8.00 a.m. to 6.00 p.m. for five days of the week and it is not uncommon for only 50% of the building to be occupied at any one time. Space utilisation of the same building could be as low as 20% and when the calculations are made which relate occupancy to $£/m^2$ it can reveal the opportunities with respect to space management which are discussed in Chapter 3. In terms of cost overhead, space usually ranks second only to payroll and staff costs and as such represents a large cost to the organisation. Any opportunity to utilise space in a more efficient and cost-effective manner must be considered. Many organisations are future proofing their real estate and corporate buildings by ensuring that the design is as flexible as possible so that the building can change, expand and contract with the organisation. This possibility of change is also being incorporated into the IT infrastructure and building services in order to provide an environment which as much as possible will be flexible enough to accommodate any direction that the organisation moves in. However, office churn (the relocation of work groups/teams or individuals requiring the change of the office environment) represents a significant cost to large office-based organisations and future proofing has not managed to stem the flow or contain the associated costs. These costs will include cabling, construction (of partitions etc.), disruption, removal costs, furniture costs, etc.. Churn rate can be expressed as:

Churn rate = Total number of employee moves per year / Total number of office employees

The average UK rate of office churn has been calculated as 35%.

Two of the more publicised approaches to flexible working and the changing workplace are:

- hot desking;

- hotelling.

The concept of *hot desking* was introduced by IBM when desks were made available to be used by any member of staff working in the building following recognition that space/office utilisation could be greatly improved. The desks were not owned or solely used by any one individual – they were available on a turn up and use basis. In the typical office scenario most employees have a desk, the most expensive piece of office furniture (the PC) and all of the associated equipment and adornments. For many the desk and associated space represents status and in some organisations – both public and private –rank is directly linked to the amount of space/office equipment and facilities that an individual has. One facet of building post-occupancy evaluation (POE) identifies 'expressions of self' (family photos, adornments and well used noticeboards displayed in the workplace) as an indication of how the staff interact and show territorial ownership of their work environment. This being the case it can be seen that any attempt to remove or restrict individual ownership and access to desks and office space could be potentially demotivating. It is imperative that any project to move to shared space with flexible working patterns is communicated and discussed fully with the team to be affected prior to implementation in order for them to get involved and recognise the drivers behind the change and the opportunity that it can present. There will be a core of staff within each organisation which by the very nature of their work are 'tied' to the workplace. (For example, surgical operations need to be carried out within the controlled environment of an operating theatre, although for particular procedures, recent trials on telemedicine have shown that with the use of new technology the consultant surgeon does not necessarily need to be present in the theatre or even on the same continent but can direct staff and sophisticated equipment from a remote control room!) To summarise, homeworking will not be suitable for all staff and all work processes in the organisation. The facilities manager needs to be aware of advances in supporting technology and must have a view on the types of work processes and staff that would benefit from homeworking. Technology is changing and improving all of the time and to keep pace there are several publications, periodicals and useful websites that deal specifically with this subject. The Labour Force Survey (1998), which was published by the Office for National Statistics, contains the following definition of 'teleworkers':

> People who do some paid or unpaid work in their own home and who could not do so without using both a telephone and a computer.

Many staff work away from the office for days at a time (such as service engineers, estate agents, sales staff, etc.) yet they still retain the desk that sits empty whilst they are not working in the building. Clearly if a large percentage of the workforce are routinely out on site then flexible working needs to be considered (space auditing is discussed further in Chapter 3). One major cost consideration is IT and support equipment – wireless technology, voice over data and video conferencing will all support flexible working but each initiative has a cost. Early schemes to implement flexible working techniques and homeworking failed because costs were not fully considered and in some cases staff had two PCs – one at home and one at the office!

Hotelling differs from hot-desking as usually permanent desk space is provided on a rotational or 'booking' system to work teams or groups who routinely work away from the office base in order for them to enjoy the benefit of a recognisable working environment.

Hot desking or hotelling will not be appropriate for all organisations or work teams and the benefits that this approaches can offer will need to be carefully evaluated in each instance. For those who work from home it is important that they still feel a part of the organisation (with access to company newsletters or intranets etc.) and that they have access to the appropriate facilities when they visit the central workbase. One big issue to consider is how does the organisation best support the staff who are working away from the workplace?

One potential downside to the homeworking approach is that staff can feel alienated/isolated and 'outside' of the organisation. They will start to miss the subtle face-to-face interactions that routinely take place within the traditional office setting – the corridor meetings, the chat next to the coffee machine and the office gossip.

Health and safety

The Workplace (Health, Safety and Welfare) Regulations 1992 do not cover the home although an employer's duty of care to protect the health and safety of their employees will still apply regardless of where the work is carried out. Most responsible employers will either carry out a home-based workplace risk assessment or will have an assessment audit tool that home-based employees can complete themselves. The assessment should cover a range of standard items such as:

- lighting;

- electrical power (socket requirements);

- fire safety;

- storage space and physical environment (furniture and dedicated work area);

- security.

LIFESTYLE CHOICES

Staff now have a whole new set of values and expectations when they apply for jobs such as where, how and when they are going to work. These may be termed lifestyle choices and they can have a deciding influence on the decision whether to work for some organisations, particularly if significant commuting to and from work is required. Companies, workers and government ministers are starting to question the accepted commuting habits adopted from a number of different angles:

- *The employer.* New technology (video conferencing etc.) will reduce non-productive time spent by employees travelling up and down the country to attend meetings (often spending more time in the car or train than they do in the meeting) Flexible working also promotes equal opportunities.

- *The worker.* Recognising the wasted time spent commuting and the impact on family life and health/motivation, flexible workers have the scope to travel when they need to and at times they choose (e.g. avoiding peak travel periods). Flexible working is also seen to be family friendly. A Telegraph survey highlighted that 56% of staff would welcome the opportunity to work more flexibly.

- *The government.* Government policy has been developed to reduce the amount of traffic on the roads (and the subsequent environmental impact) and to encourage companies to adopt 'Green Travel Plans' which promote walking, cycling, public transport and car sharing. If the rush hour peaks could be smoothed or reduced then future transport infrastructure would not need to be designed to deal with the large 'peak load' capacity which only occurs for short periods during the day.

An important point to consider regarding flexible working, in whatever way it is conducted, is how to ensure that the workplace stimulates and complements creative and productive thought processes. Where do workers have their best ideas? Are they at home, in the office, on the train? Raymond and Cunliffe (1996) outline the 'thinker's workplace', which takes account of the different fundamental modes in which people work:

- *contemplation* (reflection) –requires a quiet space away from the normal daily activity, with no distractions and physical comfort;

- *concentration* – requires an absence of distraction but for more creative activities it also requires a degree of stimulation and the opportunity to take easy breaks (this could perhaps be accomplished in the home setting);

- *communication* – requires breakout areas, formal meeting rooms, circulation space, open plan design;

- *conviviality* – requires areas for eating and meeting at work, or getting together with flexible or dispersed work colleagues over a meal to promote organisational bonding.

TOWARDS VIRTUALITY

Charles Handy's vision of future working methods includes the concept of portfolio working (see key definitions above) with more and more self-employed staff working on a short-term basis or on project work activity. They may be employed by a number of organisations, and working on a number or portfolio of contracts at any one time. This can be compared to the consultancy approach. Handy's (1989) description of the 'shamrock organisation' (see Figure 4.1) provides yet another possible work scenario for the future.

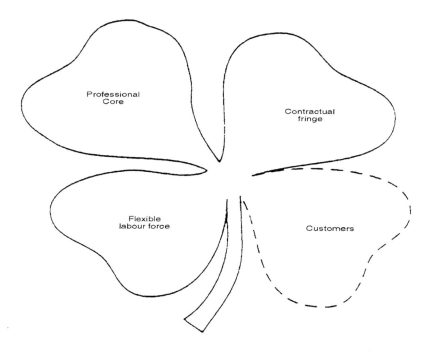

Figure 4.1 The Handy 'shamrock organisation'.

(*Source*: Handy, 1989.)

The shamrock organisation has a number of interesting applications and implications for the facilities management industry. Handy uses the three leaves of the shamrock – which was used by St Patrick to show that

the three leaves were still part of one leaf, just as the Father, the Son and the Holy Ghost are still the same God –
as a symbol of the organisation which consists of three parts:

- the professional core;

- the contractual core;

- the flexible labour force.

The professional core is made up of a group of qualified professionals who are essential to the existence and performance of the organisation. The professional core owns the knowledge which distinguishes the organisation from other competitors in the marketplace.

The contractual fringe is made up from individuals and other smaller organisations (subcontractors) who are outside of the main or host organisation and who carry out elements of non-essential work and a range of specialist services on the organisation's behalf.

The flexible labour force comprises all of the part-time and temporary workers. This group provides the organisation with labour force flexibility – staff are brought in as workload, demand and market activity dictate (i.e. staff are hired and fired 'on demand').

Each of the three categories of workforce – all working for the same organisation that Handy describes – will have different expectations and levels of commitment to the organisation.

The flexible labour force is a growing area of employment in the UK, particularly in service industries. One attraction of this labour force is that it can be used to deal with peaks and troughs of activity and to match the delivered level of service to any changes in customer requirements.

A parallel can be drawn between Handy's concept of the shamrock organisation and the current options available when packaging together facilities management contracts. The professional core represents the core business or activity of the organisation. The contractual fringe could be represented by the facilities management contractor who is running a portfolio of contracts, or a facilities management agent coordinating and monitoring the provision of contract services. The flexible labour force could be represented by subcontract labour, agency or bank staff who are hired to work on a specific project and when the project has been completed the team is disbanded. This approach enables the organisation to keep overheads under control by not having to carry, train, house and resource large project teams. However, there is a downside to this approach, such as the learning curve that is created each time a new project team is assembled, and there is also the question of company loyalty, as with this method of working staff are free to work on contracts or projects for competitors or rival organisations. Nevertheless, the concept of the shamrock organisation represents a shift away from traditional bureaucratic, pyramid-shaped hierarchies with significant parts of the organisation being made up from contract suppliers and significant layers of management and supervisory structure existing outside of the organisation. As a result of this approach organisational management structures are now becoming smaller and flatter with fewer management layers.

Tom Peters (1989: 355) describes excessive structure as 'management's time bomb and structural bloat', proposing that organisational structures should be limited to a maximum of five management layers. The current market trends of outsourcing and market testing are resulting in large numbers of staff being pushed 'outside' of the organisation. Some advantages and disadvantages of this approach are detailed below:

Advantages

- Can be a cost-effective process (if carried out correctly).

- Enables resources to be matched with workload.

- Elements of risk are transferred to the contractor.

- Reduces fixed overhead costs.

- Creates a leaner/meaner operation.

- The environment which results should allow creativity, innovation and flexibility.

- Staff who deal with 'moments of truth' are empowered.

- There is no requirement to pay holiday/sick pay, pensions, etc.

Disadvantages

- The 'big picture' view (task orientation) is lost.

- Commitment is reduced.

- The in-house skill base is depleted.

- There is no job security.

- There is no career development path.

- There is no sense of ownership/belonging.

The impact of the changing workplace with respect to space and working patterns will force facilities professionals to re-engineer their support to the organisation to meet the changing requirements of the service. The advent of 24-hour seven-days-a-week shopping, coupled with increasing globalisation and working through international time zones, will ultimately impact upon all organisations to a greater or lesser degree, and facilities managers will need to start questioning the need to own or build new buildings in this era of change and uncertainty. Again this brings the facilities manager back into the frame as the change manager controlling the interaction between people, places and processes as outlined in Chapter 1. If the organisation is moving data rather than people then clearly there will be an environmental benefit in terms of saved energy and less transport/pollution. By being proactive in response to changing social and working patterns facilities can break the traditional mould and embrace and support the new seven-days-a-week business society in which we all live. By sweating the assets and re-engineering (by posing the questions 'why do we do the things that we do?', 'Do we need to do them?' and 'How could we do them better?)' facilities can help to drive changes in the way service provision is viewed and ultimately delivered.

THE VIRTUAL ORGANISATION

Facilities service contracts can be set up or 'packaged' from a range of options such as total in-house provision, total outsourced provision or a combination of internal/external providers. The concept of virtuality is becoming more and more commonplace in the provision of facilities with companies operating a varied portfolio of in-house/external service packages. Virtual companies have been set up to provide FM services, combining a mixture of service provision options structured in such a way as to ensure maximum value for money and flexibility of delivery. The key factor to consider in operating with a mix of in-house/external contract providers (the virtual package) is to ensure that a totally seamless service is provided to the customer which does not highlight the gaps or points of friction that may exist where the internal and external providers interface during a process. In order for internal/external providers to work together strong management is required along with a shared vision and shared organisational culture and values. In an article on the new corporate reality Sam Cassels (1996) develops the concept of virtuality and draws a parallel with City dealers trading in invisible commodities and futures: 'It is no longer the case that somewhere in the chain of economic activity an identifiable product must be produced.' Cassels suggests that the output of facilities providers fall into the category of 'invisibles', stating that the major output of service industries is . . . 'service'. If this is so then for facilities providers the battle for service quality and performance is won or lost on how the 'invisibles' are managed.

Virtuality looks set to grow in the facilities field with more and more consortium teams being created to work on contracts and developments. This approach requires a pooling of the organisational cultures and values of the team members in order to ensure that a seamless service is ultimately delivered.

Alexander (1992: 1–2) states the following:

> The development of estates and hotel services have not always been aligned to strategic health care plans and to user needs. Operational criteria have often been developed in isolation from service planning. As a consequence it has not always been tuned to the needs of patients and customers.

Certainly within the health sector in the past there existed the almost arrogant view that estates knew exactly what the customer wanted and then set about developing the service based around a set of generic policies and procedures – with little or no input from the customer. This approach often resulted in the creation of stand-alone systems of work that are unable to integrate into the overall service provision and fail to fully satisfy customer requirements. Where these services are provided by contracted providers the approach destroys the seamless virtual service concept.

CHAPTER 5

Service Delivery

This chapter will briefly outline how software can assist with information exchange and facilities data collection and how Computer-Aided Facilities Management systems (CAFM) can be used. Maintenance types and standard definitions along with workload planning will also be discussed.

HELPDESKS

Helpdesks are now widely used in the facilities environment and effectively they represent the electronic interface between the customer and the facilities provider. They have replaced the traditional telephone or paper-based works request system – which required requests to be manually recorded and then entered into another system (whether manual, paper-based or a stand-alone software package) in order to produce work dockets or job requests. With the advent of improved software technology and improved off-the-shelf software packages, helpdesks have become a management tool that is both powerful and vital to the FM organisation. Indeed, the helpdesk has become the focal point for communication into and out of the facilities department and is a vital point at which to capture data. PFI service operators and all serious FM service providers operate a helpdesk system, often linked to a suite of CAFM programs which control a range of facilities data and information. Key information relating to cost, recharging, materials and performance/response times can be captured and manipulated by means of a reporting package.

Helpdesks can be set up and operated in a number of different ways but basically the helpdesk program will be set up as follows:

- Information on the site (buildings, block numbers, room numbers, GIA, floors/storeys, etc.) are entered into the program. CAD (computer-aided design) floor plans and BMS (building management system) and asset register information can also be added to the 'core' database.

- Key users or departmental contacts are entered into the database – electronic telephone directories etc. can be scanned in to aid the process.

- Cost centres or cost codes specific to sites/blocks/departments, etc. are entered.

- Contracts and service contractor information as well as in-house staff details, shift times, holidays, etc. are also added.

- Standard job types/failure modes, definitions, etc. are also entered in.

- Information on service level agreements such as response times, service standards, etc. is also included.

The above represents a minimum data set to get the helpdesk functioning.

Once the data has been entered (bearing in mind that helpdesk programs work in slightly different ways and require different types of data) the system can be used as follows:

- A call is received and the helpdesk operator keys in the following information:

  - the caller (name/reference);

  - date and time of the call is automatically logged;

  - the location of the problem (site/building/department/room);

  - the type of problem (breakdown/maintenance, catering, security, house keeping or cleaning);

  - additional information (access or working hours of department etc.);

  - urgency (as determined in SLA, specification or service charter).

- The helpdesk operator then allocates a unique helpdesk ID number for future reference/feedback or follow-up.

- The helpdesk operator produces the work request and forwards it to the appropriate person/contractor.

- The job is actioned/completed.

- The feedback information from the service provider is fed back into the helpdesk (time to rectify, spares/consumables required, cause of problem, maintenance history, etc.).

All of the information required as listed above can be collected over the telephone in real time or as long as it takes to detail the problem and key the information into the helpdesk (simultaneous operation). The helpdesk operator often wears a headset and microphone so that both hands are free to type in information. The helpdesk operator can work from an on-screen prompt list or script which extracts the data from the caller in the order that the operator enters it into the PC. Information regarding the requesting department or person is entered (the telephone extension number can be entered enabling default information from the electronic telephone directory to be automatically inserted into the correct text boxes on-screen to save data entry time).

A number of helpdesk programs are fast enough and have a front-end interface screen laid out in such a way that the request relayed over the telephone can be keyed straight into the helpdesk in 'real time' without having to delay the caller unnecessarily or having to call them back to give a unique call reference number. It is important to choose a telephone number that is easy to remember if possible for the main helpdesk number so that people can memorise it. It is also useful to 'market' the helpdesk – stickers can be attached to all internal or company telephone handsets displaying the helpdesk contact number and outlining the basic procedure required to request action or to log a request. Service charter, SLA or response time information should also be circulated widely. Helpdesk requests must be completed and the feedback loop maintained in order to close down jobs/requests and produce meaningful information. Most helpdesks have the facility to track the progress on tasks at various stages in order to keep the customer informed. For example, suppose a maintenance request is logged on the helpdesk and an engineer attends the problem but a part needs to be ordered in order to effect a repair and delivery will take 48 hours, then this information can be fed back into the helpdesk in order to keep the affected department informed on progress. The information will also allow a maintenance history on the equipment and suppliers to be built up over time.

COMPUTER-AIDED FACILITIES MANAGEMENT

CAFM systems build upon the core data that is entered to set up the facilities helpdesk. The information is used to link a range of programs, functions and activities and so produce an all-embracing electronic facilities data solution. There are a number of different CAFM packages and each one has a range of different modules or bolt-on software packages in the suite but they all usually include the following:

- planned maintenance;

- a work planner/scheduler;

- asset management;

- portable appliance testing;

- energy monitoring and targeting;

- a CAD space management/space database package;

- a purchase order/stores package;

- a finance package;

- a report writer.

Other systems include labour management, leasing/property management, bar coding, room booking, portering/cleaning tracking, supply contracts, health and safety, ID badges and access control. Others have the capability of linking into existing BMS and plant alarm programs. From the above list it can be seen that there is tremendous potential to construct a CAFM system that links key FM business activities and enables data to be generated, collected and stored in a powerful database to produce the following types of reports:

- performance reports – response time, mean time to repair, month on month comparisons;

- employee performance reports;

- an overlay of assets into floor plans to create room or work team data to assist with churn (asset details/inventory are kept on a separate data drawing layer or spreadsheet which is electronically linked to the CAD plan for the room which the inventory relates to, and if the room needs to be moved as a result of churn then the asset information can be moved automatically and updated with the drawing);

- overhead costs, maintenance per m^2, costs per department, costs per building;

- slow moving stock reports etc.

The list goes on. Usually such report writing packages are easy to use and a wide range of reports of varying complexity and presentation format can be produced as required. Some systems, however, produce a small range of 'standard' reports and new or bespoke reports have to be generated initially by the supplier at an extra cost.

A note of caution is required here. As previously outlined, there are no 'off-the-shelf' solutions to FM. CAFM is a very powerful and useful tool for facilities professionals but there is no off-the-shelf approach to CAFM either. Often these all-embracing program suites or modules are really CAD or space packages with bolt-ons or maintenance programs with bolt-ons. Effectively this means that the programs are great at one end of the spectrum but often there is a trade-off, for example the space biased programs are not so detailed at the maintenance end of the spectrum and vice versa. As a result many CAFM systems have been purchased in the past because the helpdesk program has been good but purchasers have not been able to use the other parts of the CAFM suite. CAFM needs to be carefully evaluated and procured, as it will become the engine of the department's collecting, scheduling and reporting function, and it will also be the main communication channel to customers and suppliers. The wrong decision could be disastrous.

CAFM should be considered and evaluated as part of the facilities strategy as it will require resources to purchase, set up and run and a network to operate on (this will need to be mapped in order to identify hardware requirements and locations of terminals, etc.). In most instances a compromise will be required by the FM provider to alter their working practices or data requirements in order to fit in with the software data entry requirements. The reason for this is that, while the CAFM packages are broadly generic, individual FM providers have their own unique methods of service delivery etc. and it is in most instances not possible to modify the software, or if it is possible it can prove very costly with a lot of delay. This needs to be considered before purchasing a system during detailed evaluation. All information produced from computer software is ultimately only as good (or bad) as the data that is entered into the database. The initial system set up is vital to the whole ongoing success of the system. It is important to map what is required by way of inputs and outputs, what reports are required and at what frequency. (Consider what is produced now and ask questions such as what information do we collect now? what information do we need?) Masses of data are routinely collected but are rarely turned in to useful or useable information. Often it is collected in case it is needed in the future! Be very realistic about the currency and the integrity of data – what do you need to have? what is it nice to have? is it reliable? who will enter the data? If several databases are to be combined or a number of stand-alone programs are to be closed down and the data collected through CAFM, is the staff resource in place to do it? Some companies employ temps or students to enter data – but this can lead to problems of reliability and integrity in the data entry. Do not underestimate the effort and resources that will be required to keep the CAFM system operational. It is worth remembering that CAFM cannot be entered into in a half-hearted or part-time way. The currency and the integrity of the data are paramount as they reveal all about the department. And ultimately the finance and performance information that the system generates will be put out into the organisation and form the baseline of operational activity.

Key pointers

- Consider if CAFM fits in with the FM strategy.

- Carefully and comprehensively map the requirements of the CAFM system – what area the main drivers for purchasing and operating the system?

- Consider the operational resource implications.

- What systems will CAFM link to?

- Evaluate systems carefully.

- Consider how the new system will impact upon the current service provision/process.

- Allow enough time to set up and test the system before announcing a 'going live' date. Consider who will enter the data – temps/students? Who will manage the system? Have they been involved in the evaluation or procurement?

- Develop contingency plans and back-up procedures (If the system goes down how will goods be ordered and work requests processed?)

MAINTENANCE

In many organisations the maintenance of the physical environment (property and building services) forms the backbone to the facilities remit – perhaps because many facilities managers have a building or engineering background. Maintenance will undoubtedly form a major part of any SLA or contract when it is included in the facilities remit, but facilities management is not about being an expert in all areas or professional disciplines (as outlined in the introduction) – it is essentially all about the management and coordination of three elements: people, processes and workplace. Therefore maintenance does not necessarily have to be managed or controlled by an estates professional. In many organisations the facilities team may be very lean and of necessity expert advice is bought in as and when required (this could apply to estates consultancy). In some organisations the entire range of estate-related services has been outsourced to the contract sector.

It is perfectly feasible for a personnel, HR or facilities manager with a catering background to have responsibility for site maintenance within their total facilities remit. There is a mystique surrounding the management of maintenance that it is riddled with risk and statutory obligation to such an extent that it 'must' be managed by estate professionals. Statutory obligation and risk management do indeed form key components in the safe and effective management of estate and property; however, the key point to remember if you are not from an estates professional discipline but have assumed the responsibility for the management of estates and maintenance services is to ensure that you have sound back-up and advice on maintenance, either within the FM team or provided by an independent consultant on a retainer. It is preferable to keep this advisory role separate from any maintenance contract you may have, as a sharp operator will identify your areas of weakness and vulnerability and could exploit them. However, it may be equally desirable to totally outsource the provision and management of maintenance to a contractor (in which case you will need to identify the budget and the specification and leave the management and innovation to them). In this scenario, as with other services the specification and monitoring systems that are agreed will be vital. The specification must be comprehensive and include plant asset lists, lifecycle costing definitions, schedules of rates for repair works, cost threshold levels, etc. The final decision regarding the FM package or method of service delivery will be unique to each organisation and each facilities manager. The method of service delivery will greatly depend on the size of the organisation, the scale of the FM function (does it support an in-house advisory/management team?) and economy of scale with respect to contract bundling of services.

Planned and unplanned maintenance

This section will briefly outline planned and unplanned maintenance and the basics of workload planning in order to introduce the management of maintenance.

The definitions of various types of maintenance, taken from the British Standards, are as follows:

- *Maintenance.* The combination of all technical and associated administrative actions intended to retain an item in, or restore it to, a state in which it can perform its required function (BS 3811: 1984).

- *Maintenance programme.* A time-based plan allocating specific maintenance tasks to specific periods (BS 3811: 1984).

- *Breakdown maintenance.* The operation of restoring an item to a state in which it can fulfil its original function after a failure in its performance (BS 8210: 1986).

- *Corrective maintenance.* The maintenance carried out after a failure has occurred and intended to restore an item to a state in which it can perform its required function (BS 3811: 1984).

- *Emergency maintenance.* The maintenance which it is necessary to put in hand immediately to avoid serious consequences (BS 3811: 1984).

- *Repair.* Restoration of an item to an acceptable condition by the renewal, replacement or mending of worn, damaged or decayed parts (BS 8210: 1986).

- *Remedial work.* Redesign and work necessary to restore the integrity of a construction to a standard that will allow the performance of its original function (BS 8210: 1986).

- *Planned maintenance.* Maintenance organised and carried out with forethought, control and the use of records, to a predetermined plan based on the results of previous condition surveys.

- *Condition-based maintenance.* Preventative maintenance initiated as a result of knowledge of an item's condition gained from routine or continuous monitoring (BS 3811: 1984).

- *Preventative maintenance.* Maintenance carried out at predetermined intervals, or corresponding to prescribed criteria, and intended to reduce the probability of failure or performance degradation of an item (BS 3811: 1984).

The above list could be divided into two groups – planned (programmed) maintenance and unplanned (response) maintenance. This brief outline is intended to define these two types of maintenance and to highlight the need to offset the peaks and troughs of unplanned maintenance with planned work. In this way responsiveness to the unknown and unplanned can be balanced with statutory compliance and service requirements and frequencies.

Unplanned maintenance can be broken down into a further two categories:

- normal response;

- emergency response.

Planned maintenance can similarly be broken down into:

- preventative;

- cyclical.

Critical systems and response times will be outlined in the SLA for a particular area and by utilising the helpdesk performance against SLA actual against stated can be measured.

Maintenance systems operated as part of a helpdesk or CAFM usually work on a job ticket or docket system. Dockets or requests are issued to contractors or tradesman. These will include details of the location, a description of the fault and an agreed response time – some also include an allowance for or estimate of the time required to complete the repair. Planned maintenance dockets may have the service routine for the particular service frequency printed on the docket to aid the tradesman. The request/docket will also include a cost code that will be used to log all labour costs and spares or consumables used during repair/maintenance. Goods will generally only be issued against a request or docket and they are immediately coded against the cost code for recharging purposes. Some contracts or SLAs operate against a schedule of agreed rates (costs per hour) for breakdown maintenance with spares used in repairs charged extra to contract (in theory all consumables used during a planned service should have been quantified and included in the contract or SLA). Some of the more sophisticated maintenance software systems have bar codes printed onto the dockets to enable the completed job requests and supplies requisitions to be swiped and scanned straight into the computer in order to log labour hours and materials thereby cutting down on the amount of manual data entry required. It is vital that all planned requests or job dockets are completed and fed back into the system in order to collect costs, response times, materials used and status of repair – perhaps the equipment is still unavailable as spares have needed to be ordered. The system can also be used to log plant history and maintenance frequency, spares, etc. – this is important for statutory maintenance tests for pressure vessels, electrical installations, etc. It is also important to log when planned routines have been rescheduled or pulled forward – perhaps to take advantage of downtime or a shutdown as the customer will be keen to ensure that the number of planned maintenance visits stated in the specification or the SLA are delivered.

Planned preventative maintenance or PPM is usually programmed on a cyclical basis. For example, a heating system will need to be maintained under PPM at the following frequencies:

- weekly;

- six weekly;

- quarterly;

- half yearly;

- yearly.

A maintenance routine will be drawn up that takes into account the manufacturer's service requirements/replacement frequency and any local implications (hard water etc.) and a series of tasks/checks will be scheduled against the PPM frequencies. Six-weekly tasks would include the weekly tasks plus some additional checks/service requirements; quarterly tasks would include the six-weekly tasks and so on. In order to effectively plan workload and manpower resources all of the PPM maintenance frequencies need to be entered into the maintenance program/work planner. The program will look at all of the site's PPM tasks over a year and highlight where there is a clash of routines – perhaps 20 quarterly routines have been programmed for the same week which it would not be possible to resource. Most maintenance programs have a feature that allows workload to be planned over a given period to achieve best fit with available resources plus an allowed percentage for unplanned response. For example, a maintenance department could base its operations on a ratio of 70% PPM to 30% unplanned or repair work. If this were the case an estimate of the total PPM hours required for the stated workload over the year could be used to establish the level of manpower or resources required to service the specification or SLA, with a buffer of generic working to ensure 100% utilisation of the labour pool in a productive manner. While there is some flexibility to offset peaks and toughs of demand and planned/unplanned workload, some maintenance tasks are statutory (i.e. equipment must be inspected and results documented at stated frequencies) and therefore must be completed at the defined PPM frequencies. In addition, maintenance of large boiler plant, pressure vessels and lifts will have an insurance implication and will need to be inspected during maintenance by an appropriate official.

The following steps are essential in order to effectively manage maintenance:

- Identify and comply with any statutory obligations.

- Produce a detailed asset register of all plant and equipment.

- Produce a comprehensive specification (input or output).

- Develop safe systems of work – carry out a risk assessment on all tasks.

- Identify key components or items of equipment vital to business continuity and prioritise maintenance tasks/spares.

- Develop a PPM schedule for key items of plant and equipment.

- Record and document maintenance and test results (reporting).

- Agree a process for a helpdesk or work requisitioning.

- Agree a schedule of rates for unplanned maintenance.

- Communicate with the organisation.

(Note that capital investment appraisal and lifecycle costing are not included in this list.)

RISK MANAGEMENT

There are currently around 700 safety related statutes in the UK and approximately 100 of these are of day-to-day concern to FM. On top of this there are over 100 authoritative codes of practice, with guidance constantly growing or being added to. Both employers and employees have a legal responsibility with respect to health and safety (H&S). It is essential that facilities managers (either in-house or outsourced) understand health and safety legislation and put systems in place to comply with the regulations and guidance. Due to the organic nature of organisations and FM contracting it is vital that all facilities contractors are made aware of the risks that exist on or in their contracted place of work. It is also essential that the facilities manager is satisfied that contractors comply with H&S guidance and regulations and have conducted risk assessments – a regular two-way dialogue should be maintained with respect to H&S. Routine monitoring of H&S systems and procedures is recommended and a compliance clause with respect to health and safety must be drafted into any specification (input or output) or SLA. Good health and safety awareness and practice is a critical success factor for any organisation.

The Health and Safety at Work Act 1974 places a legal duty on those who control premises to ensure the safety of employees: 'Employers have a duty under the law to ensure, so far as is reasonably practicable, the health, safety and welfare of employees at work.' It also places responsibility onto employees to take reasonable care and to cooperate with employers.

The Management of Health and Safety at Work Regulations 1992 require that any person who is exposed to serious and imminent danger is informed of the hazard and of the necessary protection procedures. The Regulations also require all employers and the self-employed to assess the risks to workers and any others who may be affected by the work that they do. This assessment of risks has to be robust, comprehensive, appropriate and kept up to date. Where there are five or more employees the significant findings of the assessment have to be recorded, and employers must draw up a health and safety policy statement and bring it to employees' attention.

There is an element of risk in all activities. Risk assessment is designed to identify the 'high risk' activities and to ensure that safe systems of work etc. are designed and adopted in order to minimise the risk as far as reasonably practicable. Each year about 1.1 million employees suffer workplace injury. This injury rate results in the loss of an estimated figure of 30 million working days at a cost of £900 million a year to industry. Add to this cost the extra costs to social security and the health service and the loss of income by the victims and the estimated overall total cost is between £10 and £15 billion per year. Properly conducted risk assessment should reduce the likelihood of workplace injury.

There are a number of paper-based and software systems designed to assist in the risk assessment process. The key points to consider when conducting a risk assessment relating to a workplace/task or activity are as follows:

- air quality and temperature;
- COSHH (Control of Substances Hazardous to Health);
- electrical;
- fire;
- noise;
- manual handling;
- movement;
- glass openings/doors and gates;
- personal protective equipment;

- VDU (visual display unit) assessment;
- trailing leads;
- sanitation a washing facilities;
- staff facilities;
- lighting;
- first aid;
- mobile work equipment;
- equipment;
- workplace–general.

Many insurance companies are now insisting on 'risk registers' that outline the known risks that exist within the organisation. These risks are then prioritised into low, medium, high enabling the insurers to calculate the scale of potential risk or liability that the organisation represents to them.

CHAPTER 6

Future Directions and Challenges

Clearly facilities management has come a long way over the last decade and there is still tremendous potential and scope for future growth of facilities management. This chapter will summarise some of the drivers or topic areas that have been outlined in the earlier chapters that have the potential for future development, or will present further challenge. This chapter will also discuss the need for training and professional development which also enables a greater degree of succession planning within the facilities management discipline.

FUTURE WORKPLACE

The impact of flexible working is difficult to predict but it will undoubtedly have a significant effect on a range of organisational and workplace management issues which currently or in the future will be part of the growing FM remit. Some of these issues are as follows:

- *Real estate.* A move toward remote working which results in work being carried out in a variety of locations – all of which may be remote from the traditional workplace – will force organisations to consider the viability and worth of owning large office-based organisational monuments.

- *IT and infrastructure.* Remote working to a large extent will increasingly rely on efficient and effective voice and data communication systems for the safe and swift transportation of data and files between locations. IT and FM strategies will need to become more aligned and intertwined as the FM may have an increasing role in managing the 'extended workplace' requirements. A corporate view will need to be taken with respect to the most appropriate system and method of working and then IT and facilities (ITFM) will be tasked with putting the concept into practice.

- *People and work processes.* Flexible working is not just about working at home. A fundamental review will need to be carried out in order to re-engineer organisational work routines and processes in order to support the new ways of working that could be adopted. Traditional work routines that currently operate on or are performed by face-to-face transactions will have to be re evaluated.

- *Commuting.* Will it be necessary for staff to spend two hours commuting to a meeting out of the office when the same event could be conducted using tele- or video-conferencing? The true costs of commuting and meeting time will need to be evaluated in order to assess the instances where physical attendance is not required/appropriate and the productivity benefits that such approach will bring.

- *Sense of belonging/corporate feel.* How will remote working impact upon productivity? What effect will the disparate workforce have upon team dynamics and organisational synergy and corporate style? Can these areas be managed?

TOTAL WORKPLACE SOLUTIONS

Space planning and workplace design brings together the need to have a detailed view of the space and space types in the organisation, and the space utilisation and occupancy patterns. Flexible workplace settings designed to support portfolio working will need to be provided as well as the 'thinker's workplace', an environment that supports a variety of thought processes and working modes – contemplation, concentration, communication and conviviality. Space management will become intertwined with 'total office/workplace solutions' which will combine space analysis with supporting furniture systems, IT infrastructure and supporting hardware in order to provide total space solutions. This could move one step on from the concept of fully serviced office space – the provision of bespoke, flexible solutions for defined periods of contract to suit project team or portfolio working – to the provision of a fully serviced/fully flexible risk assessed, IT connected 'ready to go' space solution. More emphasis will be placed upon the cost of space and the overhead that it represents as a component of the total cost of doing business.

GLOBALISATION

As traditional work patterns and routines are re-engineered in order to fully support global time zones, the 24/7 (24 hours a day, seven days a week) FM support requirement will become more prevalent. On-line support will be required for the bigger FM players who are destined to operate in global markets. The demand and the attraction of remote call centres and admin bureau services looks set to continue. (Wall street banks are already transferring data input and administration over to Australia at the close of traditional US banking hours so that admin functions and data entry can be effected overnight in order to give a competitive edge at opening time next morning – all achieved without employing extra staff or paying expensive out-of-hours enhancements or overtime). Does the FM helpdesk function need to physically reside on the site where services are provided? Economy of scale is gained by combining functions and multi-site activity, while retaining a unique site identity in order to ensure the operation of one helpdesk which runs at 100% productivity, rather than, say, four separate helpdesks, each operating at 25% productivity.

PORTFOLIO WORKING

As outsourcing continues and more and more staff are pushed 'outside of the organisation' then it must follow that a great degree of knowledge regarding how the organisation operates will exist in these outsource clusters. Teams or portfolios of workers will be brought together to deal with individual projects or contracts and will disband upon project completion. This will offer a number of benefits such as a creative and dynamic environment in which to work with a breadth of focus and challenge, but what of company loyalty – where does that go when the team disbands? On a longer-term note, how will career development paths operate? There will be fewer 'jobs for life', and while training and professional development will be very important who will foot the training and development bill for these potentially self-employed 'portfolio nomads'? Future career path development will centre around individuals developing transferable skills or acquiring knowledge and training to secure their own employability, picking up knowledge and contacts from each contract that they work on. This method of working will also require an additional set of skills to the current facilities skill areas. As outlined in the introduction, facilities managers are becoming more generalist rather than specialist. To support this working model a framework of core competencies will need to be developed covering the traditional skill base areas but supplemented to support the new skills required for the new ways of working, e.g. teamworking, mediation and 'people/HR' skills. The portfolio worker will need to be resilient, flexible, highly motivated and articulate in order to perform well in a number of different workplace scenarios.

Whichever way the FM marketplace develops there will be an increasing need to develop facilities management training and development packages and to construct a mechanism for unifying and developing the professional image of facilities management as so many current facilities management professionals consider themselves as professionals allied to their original professional discipline rather than professional facilities manager, i.e. as architects or quantity surveyors who manage facilities.

BEST VALUE/ADDED VALUE

The best value approach is currently being championed in the public sector with local government and health care. It is designed to ensure that a more strategic view of facilities and facilities services is taken and advocates the development of an FM strategy and a rolling programme or service review with a phased move from input to output specification as services are reviewed. Reliance on performance monitoring and benchmarking will figure highly in making this initiative a success. As profit margins are reconsidered in a competitive marketplace with bid prices and methods of service delivery getting closer and more consistent, the key determining factors in winning contracts will be innovation, risk/reward and added value – that little bit extra at no additional cost.

PERFORMANCE MONITORING/BENCHMARKING

In order to evaluate a best value or value for money approach to facilities services then a robust monitoring and performance system will be required. Key performance indicators (industry standards) will need to be established linked to a standard approach to monitoring so that a realistic view of performance can be achieved. A standardised approach to monitoring and performance checking should then feed directly into a recognised format for benchmark comparison and reporting that allows a minimum of local interpretation of the data to be included into the benchmarking return. The benchmarking return and the indicators need to be presented in such a way that they are very explicit with regard to the exact data that is required for the return and how it can be obtained. A more rigorous and robust approach will enable benchmarking club members to feel comfortable that the returns will enable a 'like for like' comparison to be made when evaluating service delivery. Perhaps this level of detail will need to be written into specifications or service level agreements in order to cut through the commercial sensitivity arguments that can arise when contractors are tasked with completing benchmarking returns. The performance measurement systems and the required benchmarking return information/frequency needs to be agreed up front.

Contacts/ Institutions/Societies

BRITISH INSTITUTE OF FACILITIES MANAGEMENT (BIFM)

67 High Street, Saffron Walden, Essex CB10 1AA

Tel   01799 508608

Website   www.bifm.org.uk

BUILDING RESEARCH ESTABLISHMENT (BRE) –

Bucknalls Lane, Garston, Watford WD2 7JR

Tel   01923 664000

Website   www.bre.co.uk

BUILDING SERVICES RESEARCH & INFORMATION ASSOCIATION (BSRIA)

Old Bracknell Lane West, Bracknell, Berks RG12 7AH

Tel   01344 426511

Website   www.bsria.co.uk

CENTRE FOR FACILITIES MANAGEMENT (CFM)

Strathclyde University Business School, 199 Cathedral Street, Glasgow G4 0QU

Tel   0141 553 4165

Website   www.cfm.strath.ac.uk

CHARTERED INSTITUTE OF BUILDING (CIOB)

Englemere, Kings Ride, Ascot, Berks SL5 8BJ

Tel   01344 630700

Website   www.ciob.org

CHARTERED INSTITUTION OF BUILDING SERVICES ENGINEERS (CIBSE)

222 Balham High Road, London SW12 9BS

Tel   020 8675 5211

Website   www.cibse.org.uk

CLEANING AND SUPPORT SERVICES ASSOCIATION (CSSA)

Suite 3.01, New Loom House, 101 Back Church Lane, London E1 1LU

Tel   020 7481 0881

Website   www.cleaningassoc.org

EURO FM

Postbox 8138, 3503 RC, Utrecht, Netherlands

Tel   0031 224551505

Website   www.eurofm.cfm.strath.ac.uk

ECLIPSE INFORMATION (*Facilities Management*)

18–20 Highbury Place, London N5 1QP

Tel   020 7354 5858

Website   www.irseclipse.co.uk

FACILITIES MANAGEMENT ASSOCIATION (FMA)

ESCA House, 34 Palace Court, London W2 4JG

Tel   020 7313 4938

Website   www.fmassoc.org

FACILITIES MANAGEMENT GRADUATE CENTRE (FMGC)

Sheffield Hallam University Unit, 7 Science Park, City Campus, Sheffield S11WB

Tel   0114 225 3240

Website   www.shu.ac.uk/schools/urs/fmgc

HEATING AND VENTILATING CONTRACTORS ASSOCIATION (HVCA)

ESCA House, 34 Palace Court, London W2 4JG

Tel   020 7313 4900

Website   www.hvca.org.uk

INSTITUTE OF BRITISH ARCHITECTS (RIBA)

66 Portland Place, London W1N 4AD

Tel   020 7580 5533

Website   www.riba.net

INTERNATIONAL FACILITIES MANAGEMENT ASSOCIATION (IFMA)

1 East Greenaway Plaza, Suite 1100, Houston TX 77046-0194, USA

Tel   +1 713 623 4362

Website |www.ifma.orgRoyal

ROYAL INSTITUTION OF CHARTERD SURVEYORS (RICS)

12 Great George Street, Parliament Square, London SW1P 3AD

Tel   020 7222 7000

Website   www.rics.org

EUROPEAN TELEWORK ONLINE (ETO)

Website   www.eto.org.uk

FUTURE WORK FORUM (HENLEY MANAGEMENT COLLEGE)

Website   www.henleymc.ac.uk/fwf

TELEWORK, TELECOTTAGE AND TELECENTRE ASSOCIATION (TCA)

Tel   0800 616008

Website   www.tca.org.uk

Further reading

SPACE MANAGEMENT

- Raymond, S. and Cunliffe, R. (1996) *Tomorrow's Office – Creating Effective and Humane Interiors*. E&FN Spon.

- Duffy, F. (1993) *The Changing Workplace*. Architectural Press.

- Toffler, A. (1995) *Powershift*. Bantam Doubleday Dell.

- Eley, J. and Marmot, A. (1995) *Understanding Offices*. Penguin Business.

SERVICE MANAGEMENT

- Armistead, C. G. and Clark, G. (1993) *Customer Service and Support*. FT Pitman.

- Carlzon, J. (1987) *Moments of Truth: New Strategies for Today's Customer Driven Economy*. Harper Perennial.

- Groonros, C. (1992) *Service Management and Marketing*. Lexington Books.

- Zeithaml, V. A., Parasurman, A. and Berry, L. L. (1991) *Delivering Quality Service*. Free Press.

MANAGEMENT

- Handy, C. (1989) *The Age of Unreason*. Penguin Business.

- Handy, C. (1994) *The Empty Raincoat*. Hutchinson.

- Senge, P. (1990) *The Fifth Discipline*. Doubleday.

- Peters, T. (1989) *Thriving on Chaos*. Pan.

- Drucker, P. (1999) *Managing for Results*. Butterworth Heinemann.

RE –ENGINEERING

- Hammer, M. and Champy, J. (1995) *Re-engineering the Corporation – A Manifesto for Business Change.* Nicholas Brealey.

JOURNALS

- *Facilities Management* – bi-monthly (from Eclipse Information): http://www.ireclipse.co.uk

- *Facilities* – from MCB University Press: http://www.mcb.co.uk/f.htm

Bibliography

Akhlaghi, F. (1995) *BIFM Conference Notes 1995*.

Albrecht, K. and Zemke, R. (1990) *Service America: Doing Business in the New Economy*. Warner Books.

Alexander, K. (1992) *Facilities Management in the Health Service: Planning and Procuring Quality Services*. Strathclyde University.

Anderson, C. (1993) *Facilities Management Case Study: Prince Phillip Hospital*. CFM Working Paper 93/08 February. Strathclyde University: Centre for Facilities Management.

Barlow, J. and Moller, C. (1996) *A Complaint Is a Gift: Using Customer Feedback as a Strategic Tool*. Berrett Koehler.

Barret, P. (1995) *Facilities Management: Towards Best Practice*. Blackwell Science.

Bell, P., Fisher, J. FD. And Loomis, R. J. (1978) *Environmental Psychology*. Harcourt, UK.

Bitner, M. J. (1992) *Journal of Marketing*, vol. 56, April.

British Institute of Facilities Management (1999) *Survey of Facilities Managers' Responsibilities*. September.

British Standards (1984) BS 3811: Glossary of Maintenance Management Terms.

British Standards (1986) BS 8210: Guide to Building Maintenance Management.

Camp, R. C. (1989) *Benchmarking*. Manchester University.

Carlzon, R. C. (1987) *Moments of Truth: New Strategies for Today's Customer Driven Economy*. Harper Perennial.

Cassels, S. (1995) *The New Corporate Reality: Myths and Change*. CFM Course Notes.

Caudron, S. (1995) 'Creating and empowering environment', *Personnel*, September, pp. 28–35.

Centre for Facilities Management (1997) MSc Course Notes. Strathclyde University.

Centre for Facilities Management (1999) *CFM Best Practice Survey 1999*. Strathclyde University.

Donnely, M., Wisniewski, M., Dalrymple, J. and Curry, A. C. (1995) 'Measuring Service quality in local government: the Servqual approach', *Journal of Public Sector Management*, vol. 8, no. 7.

Duncan, T. (1987) *Electronics Today and Tomorrow*. John Murray.

Eltringham, M. (1999) 'Facilties management excellence.', *FMX Journal*.

Gronroos, C. (1992) *Service Management and Marketing: Managing the Moments of Truth in Service Competition.* Lexington Books.

Hammer, M. and Champy, J. (1995) *Re-engineering the Corporation – A Manifesto for Business Change.* Nicholas Brealey.

Handy, C. (1995) 'Trust and the virtual organisation', *Harvard Business Review*, May.

Handy, C. (1989) *The Age of Unreason.* Penguin Business.

Handy, C. (1994) *The Empty Raincoat.* Hutchinson.

Hiles, A. (1994) *Service Level Agreements: Managing Cost and Quality in Service Relationships.* Wiley & Sons.

Kotler, P. and Bloom, P. M. (1999) *Marketing Professional Services.* Free Press.

Latham, M. (1998) *Constructing the Team.*

National Economic Development Office (NEDC) (1991) *Partnering – Contracting without Conflict.*

National Statistics Office (1998) *The Labour Force Survey.*

NHS Estates (1996) *Re-engineering the Facilities Management Service*, Health Facilities Note 16.

Peters, T. (1989) *Thriving on Chaos.* Pan.

Raymond, S. and Cunliffe, R. (1996) *Tomorrow's Office – Creating Effective and Humane Interiors.* E&FN Spon.

Rees, D. (1998) 'Management structures of facilities management in the National Health Service', *Facilities*, vol. 16, no. 9, September.

Schmenner, R. W. (1995) *Service Operations Management.* Free Press.

Senge, P. (1990) *The Fifth Discipline – The Art and Practice of the Learning Organisation.* New York: Doubleday.

Technical Assistance Research Programme Report 1997.

Thomson, T. `(1991) 'Matching services to business needs: resourcing routine services and projects', *Facilities*, vol. 9, no. 6.

Toland, S. (1995) *Value Management*, CFM Course Notes FM06. May. Strathclyde University: Centre for Facilities Management.

Treasury report (1998) *Setting New Standards: A Strategy for Government Procurement.*

Zeithaml, V. A. , Parasuraman, A. and Berry, L. L. (1985) D*elivering Quality Service.* Free Press.

Index